MW01241173

Published by
House of Songhay II
Washington, DC

www.NkechiTaifa.org.
www.ReparationEducationProject.org

Library of Congress Control Number:
2022922552

Paperback
978-1-7379825-1-7
Hardback
978-1-7379825-2-4
Ebook
978-1-7379825-3-1

Printed in the United States of America

Dedicated
to the memories of

**Queen Mother Audley Moore
and President Imari Abubakari Obadele I**

**The Mother and Father of the Modern-Era Reparations
Movement, whose feet I sat under, whom I learned from and am
forever inspired by!**

Fire is one of the four main elements found on Earth. It is the only element that humans can produce on their own, so it bridges the connection between the spiritual and the physical. Fire illuminates, purifies, and brings warmth but can also cause pain, damage, and destruction. It can symbolize the eternal flame of hope or signify ruin and demise. The spirit of reparations is spreading across the country like fire. Whether it heals or consumes depends on how America responds to its long overdue debt.

ACKNOWLEDGEMENTS

Thank you to everyone who prodded me to complete this modest written contribution to our ever-evolving movement for reparations, truth, and healing. Thank you especially to Todd Steven Burroughs, who provided invaluable assistance to me in helping shape my words and thoughts. I thank Oforiwa Idawa, Yao Enun, Kate Epstein of EpsteinWords, Phyl Campbell, Kimb Williams, Rodney Ladson, and Kathryn Bowser for their treasured assistance on my projects, including *Reparations on Fire.* And I am forever appreciative to my muses, Dr. Deborah Eshe Bernal (IyaNifa Ifabola) and Anuli Street, for their everlasting inspiration.

REPARATIONS ON FIRE

How and Why It's Spreading Across America

Nkechi Taifa

Published by
House of Songhay II
Washington, DC

TABLE OF CONTENTS

5   INTRODUCTION

15   CHAPTER ONE: **KINDLING!**
"They Stole Us, They Sold Us, They Owe Us": My Journey in the Reparations Movement

30   CHAPTER TWO: **FLAME!**
A Brief History of the Black Reparations Movement in the U.S.

50   CHAPTER THREE: **BLAZE!**
The Movement Inside the States: Governors, Mayors, City Councils, Laws, Initiatives, Commissions, and More – Including a Concise U.S. Reparations Initiatives Chart, Jan 2020–Sept 2022

75   CHAPTER FOUR: **BONFIRE!**
Universities, Corporations, Religious Institutions, Descendant Initiatives: Opening Up the Caskets

87   CHAPTER FIVE: **COMBUSTION!**
International Appeals for U.S. Basic Human Rights; CARICOM Points the Path for Global Reparations

108   CHAPTER SIX: **WILDFIRE!**
My Miscellaneous Musings on Reparations

118   APPENDIX
The reprinted text of *Reparations Yes! The Legal and Political Reasons Why New Afrikans – Black People in the United States – Should be Paid Now for the Enslavement of Our Ancestors and for War Against Us After Slavery*, by Chokwe Lumumba, Imari Obadele, and Nkechi Taifa (1987)

198   INDEX

INTRODUCTION

I celebrated the week of the second annual federal observance of Juneteenth the way an activist should: standing robust among spokespersons of a 200-strong national reparations coalition and getting unceremoniously thrown off the South Lawn of the White House! Representatives of the massive Why We Can't Wait Coalition of racial justice, religious, and civil and human rights groups were not at the White House to get arrested on June 16, 2022; we were there to have a press conference about reparations, to publicly prod President Joe Biden to create and sign an Executive Order establishing a reparations commission that would study and develop proposals. As the country was beginning a celebration of its new national holiday, the Coalition had a 150 x 50 foot garden of red flowers, black mulch, and green plants assembled, representing the colors of the Pan-African flag. This garden was designed to raise the awareness of not only the occupants of the White House but also the public passersby, that the enslavement era and its living legacies must not be forgotten.

I hope it was not my brief remarks that caused the security issue in the evacuation, as mine was the only presentation to be delivered in full before our removal. But you be the judge.

The performance poet in me began my three minutes spitting the beginning of a verse from one of my storypoems:

> The 16th of June, will be slavery's doom
> At the stroke of midnight, the Blacks will strike!

My remarks continued:

Those were essentially the words spoken on this day, June 16th, exactly 200 years ago in the year 1822, by freedom fighter Denmark Vesey. Unfortunately, the Blacks were unable to strike, as the rebellion was quashed, Vesey was hung, and chattel slavery continued for another 43 long years. Today, on the Ellipse of the South Lawn of the White House, we come to resurrect the demands of Denmark Vesey and all our other ancestors for freedom.

I proceeded to outline a litany of historic and contemporary abuses:

Freedom from the vestiges and living legacies of the chattel enslavement period. Freedom from the vestiges and living legacies of the black codes, the chain gangs, the convict leasing system, the sharecropping, the Jim Crow/apartheid, the lynchings, the mass destruction of Black towns, the evisceration of the right to vote, the redlining, the Black/white wealth gap, the inferior and false education, the health disparities, the police killings, the mass incarceration, the denial of the right to self-determination.

I then explained why the federal government must address the issue of reparations:

Today, on the Ellipse of the South Lawn of the White House, we come to hold the federal government accountable for its role in this crime against humanity. The U.S. Constitution enshrined the continued importation of kidnapped persons, relegated human beings to three-fifths of a white person and, most egregious, mandated that no enslaved person, even if he or she had reached a free state, was safe. That it was the duty, the legal obligation, and the constitutional responsibility of every white man, woman, or child to track down the escaped person and deliver him or her up to the

U.S. government under the Constitution's Fugitive Slave Act.

I passionately concluded:

> So that is why we are here today, on the grounds of the White House, surrounded by the red, black, and green symbol of freedom: to pronounce to the President of the United States that Black people can wait no longer for reparatory justice. That the immediate signing of an Executive Order bringing H.R. 40 and S. 40 into existence is the right thing to do on this day, at this time, to fulfil his promise to Black voters to support a study of reparations to tackle systemic racism and the continuing impacts of slavery.

I cannot say definitively that my words had anything to do with our abrupt removal from the grounds of the White House but, shortly after my remarks, our delegation, along with assembled press, was whisked away, ostensibly for security reasons. We were directed toward Constitution Avenue although, ironically, I did not feel our constitutional First Amendment rights had been protected.

Several hours later and two centuries away from Vesey's ominous declaration, we were finally allowed back onto the White House South Lawn, the nebulous security threat having mysteriously vanished. Although our entreaty to the President on the grounds of his official residence was hindered, the Pan-African floral arrangement remained on the lawn through Juneteenth, a reminder that the flowering of a new day for Black people was on the horizon, and that its bloom would ultimately bring reparatory justice.

The year before this White House fiasco, and two days after the United States' 2021 commemoration of its Declaration of Independence, blockbuster news shook up the country on the morning of July 6, making the front page of the *Washington Post* and earning one of the subjects an exclusive interview with Gayle King on *CBS This Morning*. Howard University announced that Nikole Hannah-Jones and Ta-Nehisi Coates, two of the nation's top journalists, were joining the university's faculty that fall. Hannah-Jones, who announced this Black Power move during the King interview, was to be the university's inaugural Knight Chair in Race and Reporting, while Coates would hold the Sterling Brown Chair in the English Department. (In a very public brouhaha that spring and summer, Hannah-Jones had been denied tenure for an offered Knight Chair by the University of North Carolina board of trustees because of right-wing pressure. After the board subsequently voted for tenure the day before her contract was to start, she turned down the position to essentially help produce one at Howard, publicly creating her own Independence Day from white institutional racism.) Together and with the millions of dollars in foundation funding they were bringing with them, the two professors would spearhead a new Center for Journalism and Democracy, an effort to train and develop Black investigative journalists at Historically Black Colleges and Universities (HBCUs).

As someone who is proud to have both attended Howard as an undergrad in the pre–Ronald Reagan era and taught at its law school during the G. W. Bush years, I was ecstatic. But I wasn't thinking about journalism training. I had something else to think about, an important connection I had to those two writers that I greatly valued, another question to ask. So, I took to Twitter and combined my typical optimism with my tongue placed firmly in my cheek:

> I'm thrilled!! So does this mean HU is officially giving the nod to #reparations?!! @AfricanaCarr @mariosesh @ToddStevenBurr1 May I finally say hallelujah? #BlackPowerBlackLawyer

I tweeted this query somewhat facetiously because Coates and Hannah-Jones had written two of the most influential articles to date about reparations for Blacks in the 21st century. Coates had come to fame writing about race for at least a decade for major publications such as the *Washington Monthly*, the *Village Voice*, and *Time* magazine. He included a blurb from his interview with me as part of his 20,000-word masterpiece for *The Atlantic* magazine, "A Case for Reparations." That 2014 cover story detailed the housing discrimination that happened in Chicago for decades—how banks made Black Chicagoans pay mortgages several times the cost of their homes. The piece did not explicitly call for reparations but did advocate for the passage and implementation of H.R. 40—the 1989-introduced legislation initiated by Congressman John Conyers of Michigan, a measure that, once becoming law, would set up a federal commission to study proposals for reparations. Hannah-Jones was on a career high after winning several awards for her reporting and writing at the *New York Times,* work that culminated in the *New York Times Magazine*'s 1619 Project, an extended examination of the enslavement era's impact on American life. She went much further in a June 2020 NYTM article, "What Is Owed." Unlike Coates in his treatise, she directly called for reparations. I believe that Hannah-Jones, who won a Pulitzer for *The Times* for her lead essay for the 1619 Project, went much further than Coates because she wrote in the era after the murder of George Floyd.

The idea that widely published advocates for Black reparations would be named to major, very-well-funded positions at any university in 2021 would have been unthinkable to us Movement folk in 1987 during the dawning of what I call the modern-era Reparations Movement. Indeed, myself, along with my well-educated, albeit radical, colleagues during that time, penned *Reparations Yes!,* a small, independently published book addressing the issue from a Black Nationalist framework. Decades ago, we and our ideas were viewed as politically marginal. But so much that had been in the margins began to move to center stage in the 21st century, the #MeToo Movement against sexual abuse and LGBTQIA rights being the most prominent. And then there were the new Black martyrs to police brutality – George Floyd and Breonna Taylor – and the so-called "racial reckoning" that has happened since. As a result of the national uproar over those police murders, monuments to white supremacy began to topple across the nation. Indeed, even the formerly radical term "white supremacy" now has become mainstream, in no small part due to the 2017 election of Donald Trump and his notorious presidency.

The 21st century started with reparations tiptoeing into the mainstream, but only as a popular, albeit vulgar-tinged, joke. Many of us remember Dave Chappelle's famous 2003 *Chappelle's Show* skit about what Blacks would do with reparations checks, i.e., buy pricey vehicles with cash and other examples of conspicuous consumption *("I'm rich, beyotch!")*. It was funny, if a little too stereotypical, and relegated the serious issue to nothing more than a joke. As such, I was very pleasantly surprised to see that the 2019 premiere of the HBO drama series *Watchmen* spotlighted the Tulsa massacre and the show's interpretation of the reparations that resulted from that historical atrocity. This was proof that we were in a new century, with expanded methods of expression and fewer avenues of denial. And even though mockery still exists, actress Erika Alexander's seriousness in *The Big Payback*, her documentary on reparations featuring Congresswoman Sheila Jackson Lee and former Alderman Robin Rue Simmons is, I hope, the first of many more to come.

History is in the present tense as I write. A new, updated version of the federal reparations bill, H.R. 40, one that traverses from study to remedy, finally passed the House Judiciary Committee in 2021, further than the legislation had ever advanced since its 1989 introduction, and primed for a vote on the House Floor. The updated bill was the result of the work of commissioners who are part of the National African American Reparations Commission (NAARC) and leaders of the National Coalition of Blacks for Reparations in America (N'COBRA) – both reparation legacy groups of which I am a founding member. And the energies from a multitude of new organizations to the issue, from the ACLU and Human Rights Watch to the Movement 4 Black Lives and the African American Redress Network, have both enhanced and amplified the long-standing quest for reparatory justice.

Energy. Friction. Fire.

Municipalities have been moving on their own to both study and put substance to the issue. America is a collection of cities and towns that are part of states, many of them red. The ideological battles in predominately white, predominately Republican statehouses and in similar school districts in 2021 and 2022 over the 1619 Project and Critical Race Theory, a legal concept that shows the racist permanence of America's institutions, show that there are many more fights to win in the future. America will continue to be divided over race because band-aid approaches attempting to close the racial wealth gap and cautious attempts to defund police will not solve the core problem: that whites have disproportionate power, backed up by police violence and harsh economic, political, and social sanction, over how Blacks live and die. That will only change by radical transformation of American institutions for those who wish to remain part of the system, or repatriation or separation for those who seek otherwise.

Alas, my Twitter query about Coates' and Hannah-Jones' hiring being an example of my alma mater's presumed new public militancy did not receive an "Amen Corner" from my colleagues. This book, however, is rooted in an intellectual buoyancy that is a direct result of the positive activity proliferating across the country.

Reparations on Fire surveys the spread of the Reparation Movement's multiple fronts, encompassing the local, national, and international arenas, much of it occurring since 2020. What is new? What does the international and national tell us about the local and what does the local tell us about the other two? Is the Reparations Movement now starting local and trickling up and out? What about the role of other culpable entities outside of government such as academic and religious institutions, and corporations, industries, and private estates?

This tome exists because of both the promise and danger of this moment, and because of the rapidly spreading momentum across the country on the issue. It documents and dissects a sampling of local actions that are popping up across America as the Reparations Movement morphs from fringe rhetoric to cautious acceptance in the form of concrete commissions and initiatives.

R*eparations on Fire* tells stories both inward and outward, new and old.

Chapters One and Two share my personal journey in the Movement, along with a brief historical overview of the quest by Blacks for reparations in the U.S. Along the way, I resurrect recent ancestors from my lifetime who have been forgotten or swept under history's rug, such as Queen Mother Audley Moore, Dr. Imari A. Obadele, Attorney Chokwe Lumumba, Dorothy Benton Lewis, and others.

The burgeoning movement inside the states is the topic of Chapter Three, highlighting the pioneering work of mayors, city councils, and local and state commissions in opening up the caskets in their own backyards as they grapple with reparative ways for amends. This includes personal reflections of the movements of the first state to pass reparations legislation, California, and the first municipality to use a creative funding source, Evanston, Illinois. The chapter concludes with a snapshot chart of reparation initiatives across the country.

Chapter Four is my discussion and analysis of how other entities in U.S. society, such as universities and churches, amongst other institutions and initiatives, are grappling with ghosts in their own backyards.

Chapter Five touches on the consistent appeal of Blacks in the U.S. to international bodies for vindication of basic human rights, and highlights efforts by African descendants in the Caribbean to gain acknowledgement and redress from the devastating effects of enslavement and colonialism.

I close the book with Chapter Six, a potpourri of statements, quotes, and personal and political musings.

The book's Appendix, representing my grounding past, is near and dear to my heart. It contains the original text of *Reparations Yes!*, the book I co-authored with New Afrikan Independence Movement leaders Lumumba and Obadele during the dawning of the modern-era Reparations Movement. We published several editions over the years, from 1987 to 1995. I am including here the first edition for both its historic value and as a current tribute to both unsung and (now ancestral) leaders in the original BLM – the Black Liberation Movement!

Reparations on Fire describes history in the making. It is part historical analysis, part revolutionary manifesto, and part political red-alert. The local must inform the national, and the national must inform the international, and vice versa. The public must see the fault lines clearly while there is still time to correct course. Victory, unquestionably, is certain. But we must make sure that our triumph constitutes actual redress and repair, as opposed to subtle advancement and subterfuge. With *Reparations on Fire* I am proud to bring additional value to the Reparations Movement as it goes about the necessary task of concretizing its goals and objectives and envisioning a future where Black freedom and joy can flourish. Forward ever!

Nkechi Taifa
September 2022

✵ CHAPTER ONE: KINDLING!

"They Stole Us, They Sold Us, They Owe Us"
My Journey in the Reparations Movement

I was inspired by an awesome revelation when I was young, and it propelled nearly everything I did in life. It was why I adopted an African name. Why I kept my hair natural. Why I marched and rallied. Why I became a lawyer fighting for justice. So, what is my story?

Tight hip-hugger bell-bottom blue jeans. Platform stacked heels. Huge towering African gele wrapped around my head. I had the whole look, y'all. Sixteen-year-old high school teenage rebellious me. I remember those days like they were yesterday. Racing to catch the bus down Georgia Avenue, past Howard University, to the office of the Black Panther Party. I was not a Panther. I was just a curious young naïve girl who relished sitting on the lap of that fine brother in the front office who was supposed to be pulling security. Every Saturday, I excitedly met the brothers and sisters downtown in front of the Soul Shack record store to help sell the organization's newspaper.

One sizzling hot day I took a break, wiped my brow, sat down on the curb, and flipped open the paper. My eyes fixated on the Ten-Point Program – "What We Want, What We Believe." I just could not get the wording of point number three out of my head.

> We believe that this racist government has robbed us and now we are demanding the overdue debt of forty acres and two mules . . . promised 100 years ago as restitution for slave

labor and mass murder of Black people. We will accept the payment in currency which will be distributed to our many communities.

Wow! It sounded magical. A magic way more powerful than Shazam or Abracadabra or Open Sesame. A magic which gave my rebelliousness definition. It was the concept of reparations. Reparations! To finally find an idea, one I had unknowingly been searching for, imbued me with a new awareness.

I was captivated, excited, and I talked about reparations whenever and wherever I could. Amongst outsiders I was ridiculed: "Too militant." Amongst nonbelievers I was ostracized: "Too controversial." But I was not deterred.

Sitting on the curb that day, I did not know about the massacres of Black people and destruction of Black settlements in Rosewood, Florida; Tulsa, Oklahoma; Elaine, Arkansas; and Wilmington, North Carolina. I was ignorant of the brutal gynecological experiments on enslaved women devoid of anesthesia which led to modern medicine. I had no clue about the enormous profits made by corporations, insurance companies, the banking and investment industries, and academic and religious institutions from enslavement, or that this uncompensated labor helped to prop up not only these entities but also the federal government, as well as states and municipalities.

But on a psychic level I could feel within my bones and see within my communities the trauma from the enslavement era down through the years – the ever-present cultural assault on our pride, dignity, and self-esteem. The continuing negative impact on jobs and income. The inequalities in education; disparities in health; and the unfairness in the justice system.

The 16-year-old native-Washingtonian-me sitting on the curb that day had not learned in school that reparations were paid right here in the nation's capital pursuant to the 1862 DC Compensated Emancipation Act – but the funds weren't paid to the newly freed Black people – the reparations went to the white former slave owners.

The 20-year-old college-student-history-major-me had not learned that the country of Haiti, which heroically won its freedom in 1803, was forced to pay reparations to France all the way up through 1947, long after both the original enslaved and enslavers were dead. I did not know that the British government paid reparations when it abolished slavery in 1833, not to the formerly enslaved, but again, to the former slaveholders, and the reparations payments to the white descendants of slave-owning families continued all the way down through the year 2015.

And the elder me was flabbergasted upon learning that in 1892, the descendants of 11 Italian lynching victims in New Orleans received cash reparations from the United States government.

Thankfully, I'm no longer amongst the isolated talking about reparations; no longer ridiculed or ostracized. I've been in the Reparations Movement nearly 50 years now; the magic has long since worn off, but I have never been more optimistic.

The issue of reparations is no longer fringe but is now front and center. The conversation is growing. There are now more faith organizations, sororities and fraternities, professional and social justice groups, and civil and human rights organizations than ever advancing reparations.

Congressional legislation is escalating. The state of California is engaged in historic hearings. Local jurisdictions are enthusiastically establishing commissions. Evanston, Illinois, is a trailblazer. The U.S. Conference of Mayors, the Players Coalition of professional athletes, coaches, and owners across leagues, Amalgamated Bank, and many more have picked up the banner. Past damages are being uncovered. White allied groups are committed to truth-telling. Even Ben & Jerry's Ice Cream has issued a call to other corporations to support reparations.

However, despite being on the front lines of this Movement, I humbly admit I don't have definitive answers to all the questions being raised about reparations. Indeed, I've spent the lion's share of my life just trying to get people to feel comfortable merely uttering the word. Today's Reparations Movement is not monolithic; there will be and are different understandings – that is why the federal, state, and local jurisdictions exploring and establishing study commissions are so important. So, please, don't fret about being uninformed, ill-informed, misinformed, or oblivious, but do be part of the momentum embracing reparations as a legitimate conversation.

I'm no longer that 16-year-old selling rebellious newspapers in downtown Washington with the tight hip-hugger bell-bottom blue jeans, but I still have my natural hair. I still love my African headwrap. And I'm still pumping up reparations. The woman you see today, though far more enlightened, may not have absolute solutions to the tough questions that proliferate, but one issue, one answer, one fact in my mind is crystal clear.

Regardless of what the future may hold for atonement for the enslavement era and its awful legacies, reparations is an issue whose time has come, and is fundamental to a long-overdue national reckoning of race in America.

The above tidbits were fragments from my 2022 TEDx talk on the issue of reparations, a year following a press conference Congresswoman Sheila Jackson Lee hosted with Congressional leaders and advocates on the advancement of the federal reparations legislation, H.R. 40. The April 12, 2021, news briefing, held via Zoom, was joined by over 70 members of the press. The briefing was strategically sandwiched between the February 17, 2021, Congressional hearing on H.R. 40 that featured Shirley Weber, Tendayi Achiume, Kathy Masaoka, Kamm Howard, Hilary Shelton, Dreisen Heath, and others, and what would be a successful April 14, 2021, markup of H.R. 40 in the House Judiciary Committee.

The virtual event showcased H.R. 40 Congressional leaders. Bill lead sponsor Sheila Jackson Lee (D-TX), Judiciary Committee Chairman Steve Cohen (D-TN), and Representative Jamal Bowman (D-NY) joined leading advocates for national reparations Dr. Ron Daniels (Convener of NAARC), Kamm Howard (Co-Chair of N'COBRA), Rashad Robinson (President of Color of Change), and Dreisen Heath (researcher and advocate for Human Rights Watch). The purpose of the presser was to highlight the growing momentum behind H.R. 40. I was asked by Congresswoman Jackson Lee to moderate the auspicious convening.

Each presenter gave glowing and well-deserved props to the bill's lead sponsor, who kicked off the conversation asserting, "This is not a cry for a handout. It is a cry for an acknowledgement that there has never been a response to our unpaid labor. We come not with anger, or even anguish. We come with facts." Congresswoman Jackson Lee continued by discussing the significance of a federal commission that will take a "deep dive on the facts about our history and where we are today." She resumed, "We come with a gift. If reparations works, the nation will be better for it and the world will see us as a nation that has no inability to address inhumanity."

I next called on Rep. Cohen who, after paying respects to the pivotal role the late Congressman John Conyers had played in introducing H.R. 40, expressed that "we have not fulfilled our promise to people who were brought here as slaves," and that there are "lingering impacts of slavery which we need to rectify." Cohen, after mentioning his 2008 bill apologizing for the enslavement and racial segregation of African Americans that passed the House of Representatives but failed to become law as there was no commensurate Senate companion bill, stated that we will "look forward to passing *this* bill, H.R. 40, move it to the Floor, and have historic action." It was clear that Cohen was displeased that his apology bill 14 years earlier was not able to become law as the result of an unacceptable Senate-passed disclaimer that the apology would not be able to be used to authorize, support, or serve as a settlement of any claim against the United States.

I smiled as I turned to Rep. Jamaal Bowman, then a freshman Member of Congress, to speak, as I knew his state of New York was poised to consider statewide reparations legislation. Bowman stressed that "the discussion of reparations needs to begin with assessing and quantifying the harm inflicted by chattel slavery, but it can't end there. The discussion must be conducted with an understanding that the trauma of racism against Black Americans is intergenerational." And, in response to earlier concerns raised about the Senate, he proclaimed, "We ain't worried about Mitch McConnell [the Senate minority leader] and we ain't worried about the Senate. We gonna do what we need to do in the House because this is an idea whose time has come!"

"We're on the brink of one of the most remarkable moments in America history," Dr. Ron Daniels prophesized. "And as our fearless courageous leader Congresswoman Sheila Jackson Lee says many times, 'We can't wait, because reparations is the only policy prescription which addresses and redresses systemic racism in these United States of America.'"

Human Rights Watch advocate Dreisen Heath reminded the press that "we are not so far from the era of enslavement and there needs to be transformative structural reforms." The millennium advocate emphasized, "The U.S. government has the responsibility to provide remedy and reparation for serious human rights violations and acts of racial discrimination and should do so promptly."

Kamm Howard contributed to the discussion by articulating what H.R. 40 is designed to do and how, citing the five international standards for reparations: (1) cessation and guarantees of non-repetition, (2) restitution, (3) compensation, (4) satisfaction, and (5) rehabilitation. "H.R. 40 allows for this government to begin the historic and necessary process to move this population from inherited and ongoing injury to wellness and receipt of justice," he emphasized.

Finally, Color of Change's leader Rashad Robinson concluded by asserting that H.R. 40 "is about building power. It is about translating the visibility and the presence of this moment into the power that actually changes the rules."

Over 70 members of the media tuned into the virtual press conference. I called on journalists from the *New York Times, ABC News, Politico, NPR, the Grio,* and more, each of whom raised poignant questions which were responded to by the assembled Members of Congress and advocate panelists. A thought-provoking comment came from White House correspondent April Ryan who, in a tripartite question, probed (1) what would be today's equivalent of General Sherman's 40 acres and a mule; (2) whether descendants of Callie House and those who signed her organizational documents requesting ex-slave pensions would be first in line to receive reparations; and (3) whether the panelists believed that an apology for slavery would go hand in hand with reparations.

Ryan, who admittedly arrived late to the press briefing, had missed Rep. Cohen's earlier remarks where he quoted Professor Charles

Ogletree, who testified during the first H.R. 40 hearing held in 2007. Ogletree jokingly commented, as part of his more serious testimony, that today's equivalent of 40 acres and a mule would be "a condo and an SVU!" Kamm Howard explained that when General Sherman asked Black clergy what they needed to be free, the response at that time was "land and all you can produce from the land." We live in a different time now, Howard stressed. Today, 40 acres would be equivalent to "a myriad of things such as education, access to capital, a healthy existence – the gambit of reparative initiatives that H.R. 40 will provide." With respect to the question of apology, Howard stated that apology is part of the reparations element of "satisfaction – part of returning the dignity of a people." He explained that there are three basic parts to an apology: (1) acknowledgement that a harm was done; (2) taking full responsibility for the harm that was acknowledged, and (3) a willingness to do whatever it takes to correct that harm. Rep. Cohen also responded to Ryan's question, pointing out that an apology by itself is insufficient: "there has to be a financial, economic response" as well. He hearkened back to H. Res. 194, his 2008 apology bill, emphasizing its provision that "we are committed to rectifying the lingering consequences of Jim Crow and slavery."

Congresswoman Jackson Lee replied that what April Ryan was seeking "are the very levels and layers that have never been researched, tapped or viewed." She underscored the importance of "standing up the Commission so it can do the necessary fact-finding on not only the pension issue but all the other areas as well."

Although there has been much focus on the House of Representatives, particularly since its historic, well-publicized June 19, 2019, Judiciary Committee hearing on H.R. 40 featuring testimonies by author Ta-Nehisi Coates, actor Danny Glover, economist Julianne Malveaux, and others, the Senate has not been silent.

I was pleased to be amongst those addressing a late-August 2021 virtual briefing, hosted by U.S. Senator Cory Booker (D-NJ), on strategy surrounding S. 40, the Senate version of H.R. 40, the Commission to Study and Develop Reparation Proposals for African Americans Act. The briefing itself was a victory in a string of victories that began before midnight on April 14, when the House Judiciary passed H.R. 40 out of committee along an expected 25–17 party line vote. The first committee vote ever on this proposal was a triumph for House bill sponsor Jackson Lee. Now, Booker was playing his role as a Senate champion of the legislation. It felt like a new time because, in many ways, it was one.

Booker said he was proud to have introduced in the U.S. Senate the second reparations bill for African Americans since Reconstruction. The first, introduced in the Senate in 1894, would have bestowed direct payments of up to $500 on all formerly enslaved persons, plus monthly pensions ranging from $4 to $15, but it died in committee. It was the George Floyd protests, Booker echoed to all of us, that had reawakened the country to awareness of the implementation of systemic racism "in ways that hurts us all." The goal of changing the society, he said, must begin with the "collective acknowledgement and accountability of the legacies of racism and white supremacy that tainted this country's founding – shaped literally the decisions our founders were making, and continues to manifest its long hand of impact until today." The fact that at the time of the briefing he enjoyed the support of 22 Senators showed, as Booker said, that it was past time for this proposal.

I was glad my remarks followed Booker's, because I needed to reinforce what all assembled sensed: the "urgency in the air." I stressed that the role that the federal government has played "can no longer be ignored, summarily dismissed, or swept under the rug," and that the urgent process of repair is critical toward making amends "for this shameful and terroristic era in U.S. history." I reminded the virtual audience the importance of the federal government having the major role in constructing a multifaceted remedy because the federal government was completely complicit in every aspect of the enslavement and discrimination/U.S. apartheid experience, from the establishment of the United States Constitution to current nonenforcement of anti-discrimination laws.

Nicole Austin-Hillery, then Director of the U.S. Program of Human Rights Watch, explained that the bill will give us a platform to directly deal with issues such as housing and education – to "connect the dots." It will take conversations that Americans are afraid of to get there, but the bill starts those talks, she said. Kamm Howard, at the time Co-Chair of N'COBRA, explained the Movement's two levels of pre-2022 midterm-election strategy. The first level was to try to "push Congress to its limits" – to get the legislation passed in the House. The second was a Democratic Party leadership lobby effort to get President Joe Biden to establish the Commission via Executive Order.

The Senate briefing happened only a few days after I received the ultimate compliment, albeit unintentionally, from some sectors of white America: two of my books, one a 1984 Black history children's book and the other, my 1987 co-authored book on reparations, had been banned by the Central York, Pennsylvania, school board. My books were part of a strong anti-racism resource curriculum that some teachers wanted to implement to increase racial understanding and social justice. The parent-fueled backlash against the curriculum made headlines. In late September 2021, exactly one week after the widely viewed *CNN* came out with a report about the school district's banned books controversy, the board suddenly changed its mind.

That school board meeting happened during the very tumultuous 2021 summer, one dominated by various right-wing culture wars. First there was the backlash against the massive, worldwide Black Lives Matter protests over the murders of George Floyd and Breonna Taylor. Then the attacks on the teaching of Critical Race Theory and the 1619 Project, the *New York Times Magazine* examination of slavery in the making of America. Then the public disrespecting of the Project's main author, *New York Times* journalist Nikole Hannah-Jones, via the denial of tenure at the University of North Carolina at Chapel Hill. Then, as the Delta variant of COVID enveloped America, public protests about vaccine mandates proliferated. And, as the COVID fatalities were impacting younger people, often-violent protests erupted about children being mandated to wear masks in public schools.

In 2021, especially after the January 6th white supremacist insurrection on the U.S. Capitol, anyone with a computer, smartphone or television could see that local white communities saw themselves as under siege, with social changes happening rapidly and without their privileged consent. Indeed, the modern white unrest can be traced to anger over the wars in Vietnam, and now Afghanistan. Control lost over much of the world; control lost in much of the United States. And somehow, all of that was exemplified in York, Pennsylvania, against my two independently published books.

To me, notwithstanding the impact of Ta-Nehisi Coates' article in the *Atlantic* and the turmoil of police killings from 2020, the banning of my over three-decades-old book, *Reparations Yes!*, meant that reparations had finally arrived in mainstream America as an issue. And it was a long socio-historic-cultural trip that got us to that point.

My journey with reparations began around the time of Senator Cory Booker's birth, when I was mesmerized as a teenager by the Black Panther Party's point number three. As I attempted to debate reparations as a youth, I did what many young Blacks did during the 1960s and '70s: I joined a movement for Black pride, power, and land. My home was the Republic of New Afrika (RNA), a movement that demanded five states in the Deep South as part of a reparations settlement from the United States. The RNA supported James Forman's *Black Manifesto*, which in 1969 called for white churches and synagogues to pay Black people half a billion dollars in reparations. The RNA drafted an Anti-Depression Program which called for a lump-sum reparations down payment and a negotiating committee between its subjugated government and the U.S. government, and successfully had the Program adopted at the 1972 National Black Political Assembly Convention. Later, as an RNA devotee, I co-authored the audacious 1987 treatise that graces this book's Appendix. That work was Reparations Yes! – as in, yes, the same one banned by the Central York school board nearly 35 years later.

Long before graduating from college, my movement upbringing under the tutelage of the triad of Queen Mother Audley Moore, President Imari Obadele, and attorney Chokwe Lumumba had entrenched me in the knowledge that reparatory justice was a well-established principle of both domestic and international law. Moore, Obadele, and Lumumba had consistently and boldly elevated the issue of reparations during times when it was extremely unpopular, but they nevertheless unapologetically elevated the issue in all circles and strata, whether grassroots or professional. They instilled in me the importance of not only consistency but also steadfastness in the face of opposition and hostility.

When RNA President Obadele in 1987 issued the call which resulted in the formation of the N'COBRA, the word *reparations* and the movement behind it became less marginal. The following year, the concept became smack *in our faces* real when the United States government granted reparations to the Japanese Americans whom they had unfairly incarcerated during World War II.

We in N'COBRA worked closely with Congressman John Conyers in strategically using the Japanese American reparations model (i.e., a study commission bill) in the introduction of H.R. 40 – the number for the 40 acres and a mule promised freed persons during Reconstruction. After the 1988 passage of the Japanese American redress bill, detention camp survivors received a formal apology, cash payments, a trust fund, and pardons for those who resisted incarceration. So why shouldn't we Black taxpayers who were, in actuality, helping to pay for amends to other groups, use the same strategy for ourselves?

I began speaking across the country, spreading the gospel of reparations. In 1995 I gave a speech on reparations at an N'COBRA convention in Atlanta, Georgia. I later found out a recording of the speech made its way to Pacifica Radio. The tape aired on Pacifica stations before the turn of the century – including as a pledge break fundraiser for the national radio news magazine *Democracy Now!* Unbeknownst to me, a person imprisoned in Atlanta Federal Penitentiary at the time happened to hear my impassioned speech on a radio in his cell, and quickly scribbled key information down, including his attempt at the spelling of my name: "Nikeche Tiefa, Howard Univ. Law School, Reparations. '*Democracy Now*' Pacifica Radio 89.3, 2/12/96."

The prisoner researched me, followed my writings, and nine years later discovered I would be speaking at a forum in New York. He instructed his daughter Ebony to go and meet me. That person behind bars was a Black man named William Underwood. Oblivious to the fact that it was my beloved issue of reparations that originally brought me to his attention, I dedicated years to his quest for freedom from the mass incarceration that had inundated the country. It was not until after his victorious release in 2021 that I found out about the radio show tape and saw the scrap of paper he scribbled my name on 25 years earlier. Ironically, it was reparations that was our link – Mr. Underwood was seeking to repair his life and, in that small cell listening to that broadcast, he felt my sincerity vibrating through the Black history–infused air as I demanded that America repair hers.

The ancestors work in mysterious ways. Spiritual connection to their realm is one of the marvels that surrounds my life. Here's why I believe they are guiding my path – and will guide yours, too, if you open yourself to their assistance. Led by new ancestors George Floyd, Breonna Taylor, and Ahmaud Arbery (and Moore, Obadele, Lumumba, and Conyers – all of whom transitioned before the reparations resurgence in the U.S.), the ancestors caused historic blinders to drop from the eyes of those whom Martin Luther King, Jr. might have called in an earlier time "white moderates."

My reparations activism, bearing public fruit since 2020 after five decades of serious, hard work, carries important lessons for today's activists. It's not just the cliché about struggle equaling progress, or the equally time-worn idea of perseverance reaping rewards. Because we know that all political and social friction does not result in forward progress and that perseverance may not always work. But what I have learned from my work in the Reparations Movement is this: you must believe in what you do, with all your heart and soul. On good days and bad. When you are laughed at and when you are taken seriously. Whether you are an insider or outsider. For it is *the belief, the faith* in a cause that endures, that holds forth in a solid fort existing beyond space and time, that is seen, heard, and absorbed in spaces as disparate as a 1990s Atlanta prison cell or in Congressional chambers in post-2020 Washington, DC.

❀ CHAPTER TWO: FLAME!

A Brief History of the Black Reparations Movement in the U.S.

Although exposed to the subject five decades ago, I have been actively working on issues involving reparations since 1975, at a time when the topic was not popular, was on the fringes, and was not fashionable. It was a time when one would be branded as a militant (which I was) or a revolutionary (which I was) or just plain crazy, which I most definitely was not. So, it gives me much pleasure today that some of the leading minds in this country and around the world – scholars, historians, economists, attorneys, sociologists, psychiatrists, psychologists, politicians, and more, domestically and internationally – are promoting the right to, and need for, reparations.

I am pleased to have "graduated" from speaking on the issue of reparations in church basements and Black Nationalist and left-leaning forums, to have been on the reparations circuits of law schools and universities since 2018 – speaking at Yale Law School, Harvard Law School, University of Pennsylvania Law School, New York University Law School, Howard Law School, Columbia Law School, Elon Law School, Georgetown Law School, Boston College of Law, College of William and Mary, Tugaloo College, and more. I've addressed the issue of reparations in testimonies before Congress, the Maryland legislature, the DC City Council, the U.S. Helsinki Commission, the Inter-American Commission on Human Rights, the California Reparations Task Force, and before countless professional and grassroots organizations. I don't share this to impress, but to impress upon you that both the public at large as well as government entities are hungry for information and knowledge about reparations, and that it is an issue whose time has come.

Despite, or perhaps because of, today's surge in attention to this issue of longstanding import, I feel it critical that we all understand that the demand for reparations in the U.S. for unpaid labor and terrorism during the enslavement era and post-slavery discrimination is not novel or new and did not begin in the 21st century. The claim did not drop from the sky with Ta-Nehisi Coates' brilliant *Atlantic* article "The Case for Black Reparations" or from Randall Robinson's impassioned book *The Debt: What America Owes to Blacks*, both of which galvanized the issue in different decades and thrust it into the national conversation. Talk about reparations did not start with Nikole Hannah-Jones' article in the *New York Times* or because of threads on Twitter.

Indeed, there has been no substantial period of time where the call for redress has been neglected.

Two of the first formal records of petitions for reparations in the U.S. that were pursued and won came from formerly enslaved Black women: Belinda Sutton Royall and Henrietta Wood, who successfully sued their former slaveholders' estates – Belinda in Massachusetts and Henrietta in Kentucky.

At the end of the Civil War, newly freed Black leaders worked closely with General Sherman in fashioning the concept of 40 acres which he incorporated in his Special Field Order #15, only to have the critical compensatory provision stripped by President Andrew Johnson.

Following the abolition of enslavement the U.S. government at the federal, state, and local levels perpetuated, condoned, and profited from policies and practices that continued to brutalize and disadvantage Blacks, including the black codes and convict leasing, the peonage and sharecropping systems, the denials of the benefits of the Homestead Act and the G.I. Bill, the redlining, the gerrymandering, the unequal education, the health disparities, the racial wealth gap, and the disproportionate targeted treatment at the hands of the criminal punishment system.

In 1898 Callie House and Rev. Isaiah Dickerson spearheaded the first mass-based Reparations Movement in the U.S., the National Ex-Slave Mutual Relief Bounty and Pension Association. Its dual mission was to organize mutual aid for its members and to pass federal pension legislation that would compensate formerly enslaved persons. The organization embraced over 300,000 dues-paying members, seeking compensation from federal agencies in the form of pensions for the aging persons formerly held in enslavement and their surviving spouses, caregivers, and heirs. Callie House was targeted, wrongfully convicted, and imprisoned for a year and a day on bogus mail fraud charges in 1917 for her grassroots organizing work.

On the heels of House's movement was Marcus Garvey and the Universal Negro Improvement Association during the early part of the 20th century, which galvanized hundreds of thousands of Black people. That movement also was destabilized by government forces and Garvey was unjustly imprisoned and deported to his birth country of Jamaica. One of his followers – later to be known as Queen Mother Audley Moore, born in Louisiana in 1898 – championed the cause of reparations throughout the 20th century, being perhaps the most vocal Black Nationalist and Pan-Africanist advocate for reparations during the 1950s and '60s. In both 1957 and 1959 she presented petitions to the UN against genocide and for self-determination and land and was active in every major Reparations Movement until her transition to the ancestral realm in 1996 at age 97.

Malcolm X talked about the concept of reparations in his speeches. Martin Luther King, Jr. proposed a "Bill of Rights for the Disadvantaged," which emphasized redress for both the historical victimization and exploitation of Blacks as well as their present-day degradation. Consistently, the Nation of Islam's publications *Muhammad Speaks* and later *The Final Call* demanded that the U.S. exempt Black people from all taxation as long as we are deprived of equal justice. The religious organization has long called for the establishment of a separate territory which former enslavers are obligated to financially support for at least 20 years. And as earlier illuminated, in 1966 the Black Panther Party listed the issue of payback for slave labor and the overdue debt of 40 acres and a mule as point number three of their Ten-Point Program.

In March 1968 the Provisional Government of the Republic of New Afrika proclaimed in its Declaration of Independence, "We claim no rights from the United States of America, other than those rights belonging to oppressed people anywhere in the world, and these include the right to damages, reparations, due us for the grievous injuries sustained by ourselves and our ancestors by reason of United States' lawlessness."

In April 1969 the *Black Manifesto* was adopted at the National Black Economic Development Conference, which included a demand that white churches and synagogues pay $500,000,000 in reparations to Blacks in the U.S., touted as only the beginning of the amount owed. The following month civil rights activist James Forman interrupted Sunday service at the Riverside Church in New York to announce the reparations demand from his *Black Manifesto*.

In 1972 the National Black Political Convention in Gary, Indiana, adopted the Anti-Depression Program of the Republic of New Afrika. It was an act authorizing the payment of a sum of money in reparations for slavery and a negotiating commission between representatives of the U.S. and the RNA to determine kind, dates, and other details of paying reparations. The Mississippi Loyalist Delegation to the Democratic National Convention accepted the Anti-Depression Program that same year.

In addition to those groups already mentioned, from the 1960s through the 1990s just about every militant Black organization had the issue of reparations as part of their platform in some way, shape, form, or fashion, including the African People's Socialist Party, whose African National Reparations Organization spearheaded annual Reparations Tribunals, the December 12th Movement which mobilized internationally, the Washington, DC–based People's Organization, the National Black United Front, the New Afrikan People's Organization, the Malcolm X Grassroots Movement, the National Conference of Black Lawyers, the Black Radical Congress, and more.

Broad national attention to the call for reparations for descendants of Africans enslaved in the U.S. unquestionably accelerated with the 1987 founding of N'COBRA. The spark for its founding emanated from a September 1987 conference on Race and the Constitution at Harvard Law School, spearheaded by the National Conference of Black Lawyers (NCBL). Reparations had always been part of Black Nationalist and Pan-Africanist agendas, but now there was interest from a Black legal organization, fueled by receptiveness from Adjoa Aiyetoro, a key NCBL leader.

Aiyetoro invited Imari Obadele, President of the Republic of New Afrika, Chokwe Lumumba, co-founder of the New Afrikan People's Organization, and me, along with economist Richard America, to address the issue of the constitutionality of reparations on a panel at Harvard and to discuss whether a U.S. constitutional amendment was needed to effectuate reparations. The three of us long-standing champions in the New Afrikan Independence Movement jointly concluded that there was no need to amend the Constitution because the basis for the Black Nation's claim for reparations already existed within the 13th amendment: Section 1: "Neither slavery nor involuntary servitude . . . shall exist within the United States.

. . . Section 2: Congress shall have the power to enforce this article by appropriate legislation." Our papers from that conference were later compiled in a small, power-packed, lengthy-titled paperback, reprinted in this book's Appendix, *Reparations Yes!: The Legal and Political Reasons Why New Afrikans – Black People in the U.S., Should be Paid Now for the Enslavement of our Ancestors and for War Against Us After Slavery.*

Our presentations both at the Harvard convening and in our co-authored 1987 book were replete with historical precedents for reparations, New Afrikan Political Science, and analyses of international law including our revolutionary fervor promoting the right to self-determination. Indeed, we felt the issue of self-determination for the descendants of Africans held as slaves in the U.S. to be key and central to a reparatory justice remedy. After the enslavement era Black people never had the opportunity to decide what our future would hold, with full appreciation of our options and reparations to put our choices into reality. Would we repatriate back to Africa? If so, how? Would we settle in the independent Haiti Republic or somewhere else in the diaspora? Would we accept the U.S. offer of 14th amendment citizenship into the new white nation it was developing and strive to make a multiracial democracy real? Due to severed homeland ties, would we plant our own flag in the ground in this country that we worked and built, negotiate with Native peoples, and establish our own independent Black Nation on soil claimed by the U.S.?

Our theory was that a reparations settlement must include the manifestation of each of these options through a national plebiscite, inclusive of both direct and group benefits. For those who wish to repatriate, we wrote that they should have sufficient resources to make that reintegration a reality, as well as for those who seek to emigrate elsewhere. For those who wish to force this country to respect our rights as full citizens, that option must be accompanied by transformative changes in policies and practices, closure of the Black/white wealth gap, elimination of educational and health disparities, cessation of mass incarceration disproportionately impacting Black people, and release of Black political prisoners and prisoners of war. And for those who wish to establish an independent New Afrikan nation-state on this soil, following the model of five states in the Deep South or elsewhere, should likewise have the economic resources and political diplomatic recognition to make that self-determination choice a reality.

Thus, the issue of reparations for Brothers Imari and Chokwe and myself was nothing new, special, or separate from what we had been engaged in for years as part of the New Afrikan Independence Movement, but what would come next and how it was handled was pivotal to the momentum we see today.

Black Reparations Commission President Dorothy Benton Lewis – also known as Oravouche (and later crowned as Queen Mother Nana Yaa Asantewaa Ohema), who worked closely with the Republic of New Afrika and the African National Reparations Organization – had earlier witnessed firsthand while growing up in Fairbanks, Alaska, the movement around the Native Alaskan Land Claims reparations issue. She envisioned a similar mobilization for African descendants in the U.S. I often referred to Dorothy as a "Reparations Expert Extraordinaire," as she brought a renewed level of vigor, relentless advocacy, and professionalism to the movement for reparations in the U.S. Working closely with the RNA and its Foreign Affairs Task Force, she urged Brother Imari to convene a national gathering on reparations to discuss how to increase its exposure in the U.S. and make the issue of reparations a household word.

I credit Brother Imari Obadele for downplaying the New Afrikan independence politics outlined in *Reparations Yes!* and agreeing to issue the call for reparations-loving people to convene in Washington to discuss, among other agenda items, dealing with an independent Black foreign policy, how to move the issue of reparations for Black people in the U.S. forward. The memorandum of formal invitees to this historic gathering included Dr. James Turner (Chair and founder, Department of Africana Studies, Cornell University); Sonia Sanchez (poet and author); Dorothy Benton Lewis (founder, Black Reparations Commission); Omali Yeshitela (Chair, African People's Socialist Party); Chokwe Lumumba and Ahmed Obafemi (founders, New Afrikan People's Organization); Sylvia Hill and Gay McDougall (Southern African Support Project); Abubadika (Sonny Carson); Haywood Burns (NCBL and Dean, CUNY Law School); Omowale Satterwhite (The Community Development Institute in Palo Alto, California); Dr. Manning Marable; Aisha Muhammad; Dr. Ron Walters; Adjoa Aiyetoro (NCBL); Bobby Seale (co-founder, Black Panther Party); Elombe Brath (Patrice Lumumba Coalition); MS State Senator Henry Kirksey; Askia Muhammad (Nation of Islam); Nzinga Warfield-Coppock, and of course myself, clad in the ideological armor of the Republic of New Afrika. Brother Vincent Godwin (later known as Kalonji Olusegun) chaired the five organizing meetings. Not everyone was able to travel to DC for that first meeting and, of course, there were countless others who did attend the organizing sessions, particularly many activists in the DC area, who were not mentioned above but played pivotal roles over the years.

Obadele could have demanded that the diverse organizations and individuals he summoned to Washington had to refer to Black people as "New Afrikans." But he didn't. He could have demanded that the only way forward must be "nation-to-nation" reparations. But he didn't. We all could have succumbed to the very present U.S. government–orchestrated COINTELPRO counterintelligence program that was tearing Black and progressive organizations apart. But we did not.

The higher ground was taken, and Obadele made the unifying national call for a mass-based gathering of activists not beholden to any specific ideology, and it was out of that historic September 26, 1987, gathering that N'COBRA was born, bringing diverse groups under one umbrella.

It was the perfect storm. The Black Power Movement was open and receptive to a broad-based approach to advance the issue of reparations. The Black activist legal community sanctioned the largely Black Nationalist effort. And we were all invigorated by movement of the Civil Liberties Act in Congress, which would become law the following year, granting reparations to Japanese Americans. And so it was in the throes of this fertile environment that N'COBRA picked up the long-standing mantle of justice, reinvigorated the demand for reparations for descendants of Africans enslaved in the U.S., and broadened the concept though massive public education, accompanied by legislative and litigation-based initiatives.

Encouraged by the Civil Liberties Act of 1988 which granted reparations to Japanese Americans, and in response to the dogged persistence of a Detroit constituent known as "Reparations Ray" Jenkins, Congressman Conyers expressed interest in introducing a reparations bill for the enslavement era and its vestiges in Congress. He felt the recent passage of the reparations act for Japanese Americans, which started with a commission to study the issue, would be a strong precedent for Black people.

Was everyone in this latest iteration of the Reparations Movement in one accord with a reparations study bill? Absolutely not. There were heated differences of opinion, with many in the Movement questioning the need for continued study – saying that it was time for "reparations now!" Differences are not new. There were differences within the Japanese American community as to their strategy for reparations. There were differences within Jewish communities as to strategies. I'm sure there were differences within Native American Indigenous communities as well. The key to success, however, lies in how differences are handled. Do they devolve into negative personal attacks, or are they handled with respectful discussion and analysis?

After invigorating principled debate, and an agreement to respectfully disagree by some, the majority strategic decision was made to work closely with Congressman Conyers and his staff in fashioning federal legislation. This resulted in the 1989 introduction of the Commission to Study Reparations Proposals for African Americans Act, later to be numbered during each Congress as H.R. 40, in remembrance of the thwarted 19th century promise to provide freed Blacks 40 acres and a mule. In essence, Representative Conyers' study commission bill provided the cover and vehicle to have a public policy discussion on the issue of reparations, not only in the Congress of the United States, but across the country as well.

As chair of N'COBRA's Legislative Commission during those early years, I found that the approach proved to be powerfully strategic. Its beauty was that the H.R. 40 study commission bill was a less threatening and much easier approach through which to garner the much-needed support for the concept of reparations for Black people that had been lacking in America across the country. Indeed, it was the perfect education and mobilization tool that served to fertilize the ground for later broader mainstream acceptance.

From 1989 through the early years of the 21st century, N'COBRA chapter members and supporters influenced several state legislatures and scores of city councils across the county to introduce and/or pass reparation-themed legislation or resolutions endorsing H.R. 40. In 1990 the Louisiana House of Reparations passed a resolution in support of reparations. In 1991 State Senator Bill Owens introduced legislation into the Massachusetts Senate providing for the payment of reparations for slavery, the slave trade, and individual discrimination against the people of African descent born or residing in the Commonwealth of Massachusetts. In 2001 the California State Assembly passed a resolution in support of reparations. Also in 2001, a bill was introduced in the New York State Assembly by Assemblyman Charles Barron to create a Commission to Quantify the Debt Owed to African Americans.

N'COBRA chapters throughout the country encouraged city councils to endorse H.R. 40 with the passage of successful resolutions in Pine Bluff, AK; the CA City Councils of Alameda County, Berkeley, Compton, Foster City, Inglewood, Los Angeles, Oakland, East Palo Alto, and San Francisco; the District of Columbia; Atlanta, GA; Chicago and Evanston, IL; Baltimore, MD; Detroit, MI; Jackson and Claiborne County, MS; St. Louis, MO; the N.J. City Councils of Camden, Passaic County, Paterson, and Newark; Cleveland, OH; Philadelphia, PA; Dallas and Fort Worth, TX; Burlington, VT; and Richmond, VA. There are likely others that were not captured in this listing, but it is significant to note that these legislative mobilizations occurred over two decades before candidates vying for the 2020 Democratic nomination took center stage.

The call for reparations was resurrected from the embers of the militant fringes to include Black professional and fraternal organizations, including NCBL, the National Bar Association, the National Association of Black Political Scientists, the National Association of Black Social Workers, the NAACP, Delta Sigma Theta, and Sigma Gamma Ro, amongst other civil organizations and religious groups.

Individuals started to go to the public, via writing and activism. Protesters demonstrated in the streets, holding marches and rallies across America. Dorothy Benton Lewis, Randall Robinson, Mary Frances Berry, Raymond Winbush, Robert Westley, and others wrote books and articles. Reparations advocates led by Attorney Deadria

Farmer-Paellmann challenged corporations that benefited from the profits made from the trafficking of human beings. N'COBRA's Adjoa Aiyetoro spearheaded the organization's Litigation Strategies Committee, where we developed the five injury areas for redress touted today, of peoplehood/nationhood, education, criminal punishment, wealth/poverty, and health.

In 2015 N'COBRA elaborated on its five injury areas as follows:

1. *Peoplehood/Nationhood:* The destruction of African peoples' culture and the infringement of the larger culture upon Black people of African descent in the United States and the prior colonies. Jim Crow and ongoing discrimination have resulted in a denial of our right to openly express our culture, appropriation of our culture, and denial of the right and resources necessary to be a self-determining people. Throughout this country's history African descendants' efforts to be self-determining people have been met with violence and destruction as evidenced by the untold numbers of Black townships, such as Greenwood, Oklahoma; Rosewood, Florida; and Wilmington, North Carolina – townships ultimately destroyed because of the surrounding white community's jealousy and need to suppress models that refuted their claim of white superiority.

2. *Education:* The denial of our right to an education started in slavery with criminal sanctions imposed on our enslaved ancestors who learned, and anyone who taught them, to read or write. Maintenance of dual, separate but unequal systems from slavery to the present provided an inferior education in schools with predominately Black students of African ancestry. Federal funds were often provided schools despite this dual education system – one predominately Caucasian and the other for predominately Black students of African ancestry.

3. *Criminal Punishment:* The enslavement of African peoples necessitated the development of a dual punishment system that continues to exist in the U.S. This dual system punishes Black people of African descent more harshly than Caucasians for the same conduct. Examples of the dual system were found from the period of enslavement through the Jim Crow era. The ongoing discrimination is most vividly evident with the continuation of disparate punishments for crack and powder cocaine (Black people of African ancestry are more frequently charged with possession of crack cocaine and certified to the federal system where a Caucasian person would have to possess 100 times more powder cocaine to receive the same punishment).

4. *Wealth/Poverty:* The wealth gap between Black people of African descent and Caucasians created during the enslavement of African peoples has been sustained; confiscation of land and other forms of wealth continue up to present day. Black people of African descent were forced into poverty through enslavement, Jim Crow, and continuing discrimination in employment, housing, and other economic areas.

5. *Health:* The focus is on physical and mental health. Health knowledge of enslaved Africans was appropriated and enslaved Africans functioned as non-paid health care providers for others; Black people of African descent were used as subjects for torturous health experiments (e.g., the Tuskegee Syphilis Study); and Black people of African descent were denied quality health care during and post-slavery. The health injury area also includes the continuing discrimination in the provision of health care, including the disproportionately higher rate of closures of hospitals serving Black communities; lack of access to health insurance to provide affordable access to health care; the failure to validate health care protocols for Black people of African descent; and the failure to provide the appropriate

medical treatment for critical health care symptoms which have resulted in higher rates of death for Black people of African descent compared to Caucasians exhibiting these symptoms. Finally, this injury area includes an examination of post-slavery stress syndrome, a developing area of investigation by Black mental health professionals of African descent.

The strategy advanced by N'COBRA over 30 years ago achieved its goal of making reparations a household word, largely due to the tenacity of early N'COBRA leaders such as Dorothy Lewis, Johnita Obadele, Kalonji (Vince Godwin) and Kupenda Olusegun, Adjoa Aiyetoro, Kibibi Tyehimba, this author, and many, many more. It is now past time to bring that household word into reality.

I am also a proud member of the inaugural cohort of Commissioners of the National African American Reparations Commission. The group, convened by Dr. Ron Daniels, President of the Institute of the Black World 21st Century, revisited the strategy of the 1989 Reparations Study Commission bill and proposed to Congressman Conyers that the legislation be updated from a mere study to a remedy bill. This effort was conceived of and led by my fellow Commissioner Kamm Howard, then Co-Chair of N'COBRA. Thus, in 2016, H.R. 40 was revised to also incorporate the actual development of reparation proposals, now titled the Commission to Study and Develop Reparation Proposals for African Americans Act.

After the retirement of Congressman John Conyers, the bill's reins were picked up by Congresswoman Sheila Jackson Lee, whose tenacity catapulted the legislation's co-sponsors to an all-time high, engineered a momentous hearing in the House Judiciary Committee, and successfully moved the bill out of committee, primed for a vote on the House Floor. H.R. 40 achieved a whopping 217 committed votes as of September 2022, testament to the dogged persistence of then N'COBRA Legislative Commission Co-Chair Kennis Henry, Dreisen Heath of Human Rights Watch, and Raina Batrice of Batrice and Associates. A companion legislative bill, S. 40, was introduced in the Senate by Cory Booker. State and local governments began to take center stage in the fight for reparations.

Following the ascendancy of Donald Trump to the U.S. presidency, worldwide attention to the murder of George Floyd and the re-normalization of white supremacy, 2020 Presidential candidates for the Democratic nomination became vocal on the issue of reparations and a proliferation of new organizations and reparations initiatives emerged on the scene. These included Black-led organizations, allied organizations, faith-based groups, descendant advocacy initiatives, and more. The Movement for Black Lives incorporated the issue of reparations as part of its platform. Unfortunately, and reminiscent of past COINTELPRO tactics, Internet-savvy groups began engaging in behavior and tactics criticized by many as disruptive and divisive.

A plethora of major faith-based entities passed resolutions on the issue of reparations, including, but not limited to, the National Council of Churches, the United Church of Christ, dioceses of the Episcopal Church, the Religious Action Center of Reform Judaism, the Union for Reform Judaism, Network Lobby for Catholic Social Justice, and more. The Virginia and Princeton Theological Seminaries, as well as the Jesuits, also earmarked monies. In November 2021 the Virginia Episcopal Diocese agreed to spend $10 million on reparations because of the church's moral complicity. The U.S. Conference of Mayors has endorsed reparations, along with Amalgamated Bank and the Players Coalition of professional athletes, coaches, and owners across leagues. Ben & Jerry's Ice Cream has issued a challenge to other corporations to step up to the plate in vocal support of reparations.

Since 2020, reparations at the state and local levels have taken center stage. California established a state-wide Reparations Commission Task Force, patterned largely after H.R. 40, which is currently engaged in historic hearings. Evanston, Illinois, has earmarked monies from its legal cannabis industry to fund reparations initiatives in the city. Chicago passed a reparations ordinance for victims of police torture in 2015, and since 2020, jurisdictions across the country have passed legislation or ballot initiatives establishing reparations commissions, task forces, or official pronouncements to examine the history of the enslavement era and its vestiges in their own backyards and think about repair. Examples include the cities of Asheville, Carrboro, and Durham, NC; Providence, RI; Amherst and Boston, MA; St. Paul, MN; Denver, CO; Detroit, MI; Los Angeles, Sacramento, and Stockton, CA; Austin, TX; Tallahassee, OK; Burlington, VT; Greenbelt, MD; Kansas City, MO, the District of Columbia, and more. Slavery Disclosure Ordinances have been enacted in 16 jurisdictions, revealing historical ties to the enslavement era by financial institutions.

Although my primary focus is obtaining reparations for the enslavement era and its living legacies impacting Black people in the U.S., it is important to recognize that the pursuit for reparations in the U.S. is also part of the international movement for reparations. The descendants of Africans living in Canada, Barbados, Haiti, Jamaica, Brazil, and other areas of the diaspora are also due reparations from their particular European colonizer. Colonized African countries are due reparations as well, as are subjugated African descendants living in Europe. As such, I have worked closely with supporters of reparations throughout the world, recognizing that the success of the movement for reparations for diasporic Africans anywhere advances the movement for reparations by Africans and African descendants everywhere.

I am thrilled that my quest to have reparations seen as a legitimate concept for Black people, beginning in those early-'70s teen years, is today becoming a reality. And while I wholeheartedly agree that cash payments remain an important and necessary component of any claim for damages, my mantra is, "the harms from the enslavement era and beyond were multi-faceted, thus the remedies must be so as well. A reparations settlement can be fashioned in as many ways as necessary to equitably address the countless manifestations of injury sustained from the enslavement era and its continuing vestiges and living legacies that collectively comprise a crime against humanity."

It is critical that we create and power our own stories and narratives. As such, decades prior to popular international articulations about reparations, I cobbled together the following definition, utilizing it in my many speeches and writings:

Reparations are forms of compensation provided to those who have suffered human rights abuses or other forms of widespread systemic injustices, or to their descendants, usually in the aftermath of war, enslavement, or other forms of gross injustice. It is the act or process of repairing or restoring. In the context of Black people in the U.S., I submit the quest for reparations essentially constitutes four elements:

1) The formal acknowledgment of historical wrong and an official unfettered apology for the dehumanization and atrocities of the enslavement era and its vestiges and living legacies. The term unfettered is critical. Symbolic resolutions were passed by the House of Representatives and the Senate apologizing for enslavement and Jim Crow. However, the 2009 bill passed by the Senate contained a disclaimer that the apology could not be used to support a legal claim against the U.S.

2) The recognition that the injury has continued throughout the years, and still manifests today. This provision is pertinent. The harms did not end with the 13th amendment in 1865. The harms from the enslavement era and its living legacies are generational, continuing today.

3) The commitment to redress by the federal government which sanctioned the enslavement and subsequent vestiges, and by states, cities, corporations and industries, academic and religious institutions, and private estates which continued the injustices and enjoyed unjust enrichment.

4) The actual compensation/redress, in whatever form or forms are agreed upon. Agreement is pertinent. It is unacceptable for the offending party to dictate the terms of the redress.

Shortly after the turn of the 21st century, the United Nations General Assembly formally addressed the issue of reparations in its December 16, 2005, "Basic Principles and Guidelines on the Right to a Remedy and Reparation for Victims of Gross Violations of International Human Rights Law and Serious Violations of International Humanitarian Law." That Resolution identified five standards that any effective reparations settlement should include: restitution, compensation, rehabilitation, satisfaction, and guarantees of non-repetition.

Restitution, wherever possible, should restore the victim to the original situation before the gross violation of international human rights law or serious violations of international humanitarian law occurred. Restitution was defined to include restoration of liberty; enjoyment of human rights, identity, family life, and citizenship; return to one's place of residence; restoration of employment; and return of property.

Compensation was cited as any economically assessable damage, as appropriate and proportional to the gravity of the violation and the circumstances of each case. Such damages were described to include physical or mental harm, lost opportunities, loss of earnings and earning potential, moral damage, and costs for services.

Rehabilitation was defined to include medical and psychological care, and legal and social services.

Satisfaction entailed the cessation of continuing violations, truth-telling, search for the disappeared and the identities of the abducted, assistance in the recovery, identification and reburial of bodies, restoration of dignity and reputation, public apology and acceptance of responsibility, sanctions against liable parties, commemorations and tributes to victims, and truthful accountings of harms.

Finally, the UN Resolution asserts that Guarantees of Non-Repetition should include effective civilian control of military and security forces and that they abide by international standards; an independent judiciary; protection of those media and legal and health-care professions; law enforcement training, codes of conduct and human rights education; prevention and monitoring of social conflicts; and review and reform of laws that contribute to or allow gross violations of human rights.

These very helpful worldwide standards for reparations are increasingly becoming part of the domestic U.S. reparations nomenclature. And as African descendants worldwide evolve in our understandings of what reparatory justice means for us, such definitions will necessarily be refined, honed, and tiered to our respective realities.

I am proud to be part of a very specific reparations genealogy, having sat at the feet of Black radical activist legends. Queen Mother

Audley Moore has been crowned as the undisputed Mother of the modern-era Reparations Movement in the U.S. Although the genius and role RNA President Imari Obadele played is largely absent from the popular annals of reparations lore, he has been publicly acknowledged as the Movement's Father. And the many contributions of my colleague, now ancestor, Dorothy Benton Lewis, a quiet and humble reparations advocate hailing from Alaska and also crowned as a Queen Mother, has yet to be written.

I consciously and consistently uplift the memories and call out the names in libation of a few of the reparationist luminaries I worked with, now ancestors, who fanned the flames for the dynamism we see today: Queen Mother Moore, Imari Obadele, Chokwe Lumumba, and Dorothy Lewis; as well as remembrances of the reparationist spirits of Belinda Sutton Royall, Henrietta Wood, Callie House, Isaiah Dickerson, Marcus Garvey, Elijah Muhammad, Reparations Ray Jenkins, Chokwe Lumumba, Ahmed Obafemi, Christopher Alston, Dara Abubakari, Charshee McIntyre, Hannibal Afrik, Njeri Alghanee, Kalonji Olusegun, Kwame Afoh, Milton McGriff, Ronald Walters, Herman Ferguson, Omowale Kefing, Earline Arikpo, Nia Kuumba, Marilyn Killingham, Conrad Worrill, Hodari Ali, Askia Muhammad, MA State Senator Bill Owens, Congressman John Conyers, and so many countless others, most of whom may not have graced the pages of history books, but upon whose ancestral shoulders we firmly stand in our long-standing pursuit for reparatory justice.

CHAPTER THREE: BLAZE!

The Movement Inside the States: Governors, Mayors, City Councils, Laws, Initiatives, Commissions and More – Including a Concise U.S. Reparations Initiatives Chart, Jan 2020–Sept 2022

Skeptics have told me for decades that I'm fighting a lost cause. Any Google News search between 2020 and 2022 would show how wrong the naysayers are, since a new phase in the struggle is both strong and visible: statehouses have become the new battleground in the national fight for reparations. They are standing on the shoulders of earlier smoldering local legislative initiatives – city councils between 1990 and 2002 that passed resolutions in support of H.R. 40 within the states of Arkansas, California, Georgia, Illinois, Maryland, Michigan, Mississippi, Missouri, New Jersey, Ohio, Pennsylvania, Texas, Vermont, Virginia, and the District of Columbia. These embers from 20 years earlier are now being reignited, encompassing over 50 cities and towns across the country.

Current actions are fast-moving. I delivered a keynote address on reparations before the New Jersey State NAACP Conference in 2021, where I cheered on serious activists such as Ryan Haygood, President and CEO of the New Jersey Institute for Social Justice and a leader of the struggle for New Jersey state-wide reparations legislation. During the conference, Haygood outlined several times how deep the historical agony echoes. New Jersey's individual net wealth racial disparity, with Blacks only having a pittance of $179 net worth in one of the wealthiest states in the United States, is tied to the legacy of slavery, he explained; whites who had slaves were given significant amounts of land by the state. Haygood's summary: colonial land distribution to white slavers through the enslavement era, Black sharecropping after the Civil War, and racial discrimination against Blacks from the post–World War II G.I. Bill shaped New Jersey through the contemporary racial red-lining that created the late 20th-century racially segregated urban cities like Newark and Paterson. He gave another current example: in New Jersey, Black youth are 21 times as likely to be incarcerated as the state's white children of the same age. As of August 2022, the New Jersey State Reparations Bill A938 is pre-filed for introduction in the 2022–2023 New Jersey legislative session.

The state of New York is also pushing hard to pass reparations legislation. Former New York State Representative Charles Barron attempted for decades to place revolutionary consciousness into policy, originally introducing reparations legislation for state consideration. Barron, Haygood, and others are attempting to push state legislatures into doing the right thing. Barron's New York State Community Commission on Reparations Bill A2619A passed the State Assembly and, as of September 2022, awaits reintroduction and a State Senate vote, with Senator Jabari Brisport and Assemblywoman Michaelle Solages now at the helm.

As the chart at the close of this chapter shows, legislative and administrative initiatives are spreading across the country at breakneck speed. Much of the attention has been focused on California, the first state to pass reparations legislation; and the first municipality, Evanston, Illinois. I have been both observer and participant in these exciting initiatives.

There are pockets of reparations work – *national*, in the form of Congressmembers, Democratic Presidential candidates, prominent journalists, academics, and elite institutions; and *local*, in the form of city council politicians and pro-reparations community organizers. Largely missing are state officials, for the obvious partisan reasons. California is now a sizzling exception to that rule.

The Golden State has stridently snatched a home court advantage in establishing the first state-wide commission to study and develop reparation proposals. Assembly Bill 3121, proposed by then-Assemblywoman Shirley Weber, was initiated in 2020 pursuant to legislation signed by Governor Gavin Newsom in the wake of international attention to the murder of George Floyd. The commission, titled the California Reparations Task Force, is instrumental, not only for the state's residents, but for the country as a whole, in that it can impart both constructive as well as cautionary guidance for the larger Reparations Movement.

The Task Force elicited significant public comment and testimony as to harms emanating from the enslavement era and its living legacies down through today. The Othering and Belonging Institute at the University of California at Berkeley has compiled much of the Task Force's collection of presentations and testimonies and categorized them into five topics: Reparations Efforts, Structural Racism, Impacts on Health, Economic Disparities, and Urban Development. Task Force testimonies ranged from slavery and systemic racism to housing and education segregation; from discrimination in technology to entertainment arts/culture and sports; and from political disenfranchisement to the wealth gap; amongst other pertinent themes.

The pioneer work of the California Reparations Task Force provides both constructive as well as cautionary guidance for a federally chartered task force pursuant to H.R. 40 and S. 40 via Executive Order, as well as the myriad of local jurisdictions and states looking at the issue.

Positives include the realization that reparations can in fact happen, and in our lifetimes, and that its implementation will greatly improve the conditions of Black people. Areas of caution include unduly shaping the nascent reparations narrative and the inability to control gross indecorum as part of the process. Indeed, as the result of COVID, hearings during the first year of the Task Force were conducted virtually. I was both saddened and shocked at the apoplectic level of venom circulating uncontrolled in the public chat area of the virtual forum. The oft-profane malice, directed specifically against anyone publicly disagreeing with "the party line" or anyone "off-code," discouraged many from participating in the hearings and/or providing critical public comment. Indeed, I generally refrained from sharing in the chat as the result of the free-flowing negativity directed against myself and organizations such as N'COBRA and NAARC that I helped to found and with which I remain associated.

Perhaps the most controversial aspect stemming from the Task Force as it was completing its first year was the heated discussion and debate surrounding what standard would be used to determine qualification for California-based reparations. One argument, buttressed by testimony from the bill's sponsor, was that California adopt a lineage-based standard, which would limit eligibility to those who could prove ancestry back to free or enslaved people living in California prior to the end of the 19th century. This approach would also narrow remedy for the lingering impact of the enslavement era on African Americans today.

The countervailing viewpoint was a more inclusive one – that a reparations package should be available to all Black people in the state regardless of proof of lineage, including Caribbean and African people.

After considerable discussion and heated debate, a razor-slim 5-4 majority recommended limiting eligibility to those who can successfully trace their lineage to an ancestor from the enslavement era.

I submit that this approach, while arguably making sense directly following the enslavement era, is formidable based on the unconscionable passage of time almost 200 years later, risking being grossly underinclusive, discriminatory, and divisive. Indeed, such proof requirement likely necessitates invasive scrutiny of not only likely incomplete 19th and 20th century records of births, deaths, taxes, census reports, and property records, but also intrusive genetic DNA tests and attempts to define intra-racial biology. Moreover, other hindrances include the reality of faulty oral histories and the changing of family names and differences in names' spellings since the 19th century. Another critical hindrance is the fact that many Blacks fled the South, taking great measures to alter their previous identities, due to abandonment of former slave names, escape from the Ku Klux Klan and other white vigilantes, or other acts of self-determination.

Being denied of heritage for so long, it is indeed laudable that Blacks scrutinize their ancestry, if they choose to do so. However, to legally demand all do so as a perquisite to qualify for a reparations benefit is unacceptable, particularly given the obstacles mentioned above. Indeed, given the concerns many in the Black community have demonstrated against state-driven COVID-19 mask mandates and vaccines – ranging from caution to virulent hostility – it is difficult to believe there will be widespread acceptance of physically invasive and/or lack of privacy-ridden requirements in order to qualify for reparations.

Cultural anthropologist Jessica Ann Mitchell Aiwuyor testified before the California Reparations Task Force. During her expert testimony she explained difficulties associated with lineage-based proof and asserted that reparations be implemented through a streamlined non-invasive approach that gives as many African Americans as possible the opportunity to receive remedies. Strict mechanisms of approval that would force families to take DNA tests and endure extensive genealogical background searches should be avoided, she stated. This would be an imposing, time-consuming, and costly strategy that potentially excludes African American families that decline to submit DNA or refuse genealogical background searches. Furthermore, she cautioned that the assertion that everyone can or will trace this ancestry does not account for accessibility and/or disability issues.

Attorney Adjoa Aiyetoro likewise testified before the California Reparations Task Force. She emphasized:

> People who look like me, but are not descended from enslaved Africans, suffer the injuries of the legacies of slavery. That is the major crime of slavery and its legacies – it imprinted on peoples who look like me a presumption of inferiority, a presumption of criminality, a presumption of loose morals, a presumption that leads to being unable to obtain jobs and housing of the same caliber of whites. Money reparations to only those who meet a burden of proof of descending from an enslaved African leave those who are victimized by the legacy of slavery with an injury without a remedy.

I was invited to testify before the Task Force to specifically address the history of the Reparations Movement in the U.S. Much of my historical reflection from that testimony is included in Chapter Two. As stated earlier, one of the historical tidbits I stressed in my testimony was the fact that not everyone was in accord with the strategy recommended by Congressman John Conyers of a reparations study bill. I restated that there were heated differences of opinion, with many in the Movement questioning the need for continued study – that it was time for "reparations now!" With the knowledge of current splinters in the Reparations Movement, I stressed that the African American community was not monolithic and that differences in strategy and approach were not new. There were differences within the Japanese American community as to their strategy for reparations. There were differences within Jewish communities as to strategies. The key to success, I repeated, was in how differences are handled. "Do they devolve into negative personal attacks," I testified, "or are they handled with respectful discussion and analysis?" I wanted that point to sink in, particularly given the seemingly fanatical level of zealousness that has risen within the Reparations Movement over the past few years and the unfortunate manner in which such antagonism has played out in California.

I did not address the issue of eligibility for reparations as part of my testimony because I am still developing my philosophy and opinions on the subject. I do feel that Black people should not be pigeon-holed into an underinclusive class of eligibility for reparations; that a more fair and just approach should be an inclusive framework that does not punish those who, through no fault of their own, cannot supply the requisite proof of lineage.

As such, but admittedly without the benefit of collective dialogue and analysis, I now proffer the following criteria for consideration and discussion:

> All people recorded as Black in the 1970 Census (the first census after passage of the 1964 Civil Rights Act and the 1965 Voting Rights Act when the most egregious racially discriminatory laws were ostensibly eradicated), and their descendants, will be eligible for direct (cash) reparation payments in the U.S., at an amount determined by the official commission or task force studying and developing reparations proposals. Such period encompasses both the enslavement and Jim Crow/U.S. apartheid eras, with

their attendant health, wealth, educational, cultural and punishment atrocities, abuses, and disparities, as well as the obliteration of the right to self-determination of a political future.

All Blacks, including those described above as well as those entered into the U.S. Census after 1970, will be eligible for community/group/collective reparations in whatever form or forms are determined by the official commission or task force studying and developing remedies. This is in recognition of the continuing harms, living legacies and new manifestations emanating from the enslavement and Jim Crow/U.S. apartheid eras and also expressly including the era of mass incarceration, which manifested post-1965.

The above eligibility approach relates to the federal level only. Because there are different circumstances based on the unique histories in states and cities, no one redress effort fits all. Also, this method does not negate specific descendant-based reparatory justice claims to be addressed on a case-by-case family/neighborhood/or community basis and adjudicated as such.

The California Reparations Task Force is chaired by Kamilah Moore, who serves on the advisory board of the National Assembly of American Slavery Descendants, a grassroots organization focused on reparations. As a Columbia University law student in 2019, she invited me to keynote a reparations event at Columbia Law School. Little did I know that the following year she would chair the first state Reparations Task Force in the country. My lecture, titled "Let's Have a Conversation About Reparations," was so well received that the *Columbia Journal of Race and Law* requested permission to publish it. I gladly accepted, particularly as the law students copiously researched and inserted citations and annotations into my speech, which was printed essentially verbatim.

In a note introducing the article I expressed I was "especially grateful to Kamilah Moore for organizing this important event." On another occasion I was invited by Moore to join a discussion she was hosting on the social media platform Clubhouse, about my memoir that had been recently published as well as the issue of reparations. I was initially reluctant to agree, as I had previously heard that the platform was negative to reparations groups I had been associated with. She assured me, however, that she would make sure the environment was respectful. She graciously kept her word. I know that there are unpleasant and polarized perspectives on the first state-based Task Force in the country, as well as amongst groups following the proceedings, but I will never forget my previous interactions with the Task Force's chair. And that is what matters: the humanness of our humanity, rather than the politics of division.

The other member of the Task Force I have a prior connection with is my colleague Dr. Cheryl Grills, who was appointed by Governor Gavin Newsom. I fondly remember Dr. Grills from her leadership of the Association of Black Psychologists, the Community Healing Network, and its Emotional Emancipation Circles. The people of California should feel blessed that she was named to the Task Force because she brings, in her own words upon her appointment, "the tools of psychology to the reparations discourse to ensure that our mental health and well-being as individuals and as a community are a central part of the process of repair." Since being on the Task Force, she has also been appointed as a Commissioner to the National African American Reparations Commission, where I also sit. I have found Dr. Grills to be courteous, measured, and professional in the face of hurtful and hostile disrespect and indecorum from external forces opposed to her viewpoints and votes on the Task Force. However, despite stark divisions on the California Reparations Task Force, it is nevertheless the first in the country to study and develop reparation proposals for African Americans, and other states are scrutinizing it as a model to embrace, modify, or discard.

In June 2022, the Task Force released its preliminary report for the public to review, containing recommendations for future deliberation. I smiled widely as I perused the voluminous nearly 500 pages and, upon reading the document in depth, remained largely impressed, with some minor caveats. I was awed by the richness of the document's breadth, but it still stung that a state had beaten the federal government to the finish line.

The Interim Report's findings and recommendations addressed areas of enslavement, racial terror, political disenfranchisement, housing segregation, separate and unequal education, racism in environment and infrastructure, pathologizing Black families, control over creative cultural and intellectual life, stolen labor and hindered opportunity, an unjust legal system, mental and physical harm and neglect, the wealth gap, and the establishment of a Cabinet-level Secretary position over a "California African American Freedmen Affairs Agency." The Report purports to overcome the obstacles I cited earlier regarding proof of ancestry with the establishment of an Office of Genealogy within the proposed Freedmen Affairs Agency that would provide cost-free genealogical research by professional certified genealogists to assist vulnerable populations within the African American community in proving their eligibility for reparations. However, I submit that problems remain with this attempt to quell dissent to mandated proof. The state funds necessary to implement such a schema could and should be put toward reparative remedies, as opposed to fueling the financial pockets of what will likely be the next huge cottage industry. In essence, we risk using African, Caribbean, and Black ancestry and genealogy to divide when we should be using such connections to unify.

The Report cited that the California African American Freedmen Affairs Agency would also be responsible for oversight and implementation throughout the state of reparation recommendations from the Task Force. Inexplicitly, the only aspect of the nearly

500-page Interim Report that called for the implementation of a "detailed program of reparation for African Americans" was in the section dubbed "The Wealth Gap." Unfortunately, that section did not discuss how closing that gap will in any way change America's power dynamic. Blacks are not powerless just because they don't have wealth; they are powerless because they do not control the political and social levers of American power – the political parties, the banks, the state legislatures. Although the lion's share of the Interim Report details harms in each section, the specificity of only calling for a "detailed program of reparations" in the Wealth Gap section leaves one with the impression that area is the only one to seriously qualify for reparations.

Also lacking (at least in the Interim Report) is an absence of discussion and analysis of the five key components a reparations settlement should include that I discussed earlier, as outlined by the UN General Assembly: Cessation and Guarantees of Non-Repetition, Restitution, Compensation, Satisfaction and Rehabilitation.

Moreover, the Interim Report, while outstandingly comprehensive, ventured far beyond the borders of California, addressing issues in the country as a whole – measures that would be and should have been the province and scrutiny of the federal government. However, no matter how disappointed I am that the federal bill H.R. 40 or an equivalent Executive Order has yet to become law, the comprehensiveness of California's Interim Report should not be blamed for the failure of national leaders to act for over 30 years. Indeed, given California's directive pursuant to AB 3121 to "study the institution of slavery and its lingering negative effects on living African Americans, including descendants of persons enslaved in the United States and on society," how could the state have accomplished its mandate otherwise?

The advent of the Biden administration should have resulted in optimism, but two years have come to a close without passage of a voting rights bill or any significant ink on police reform, much less H.R. 40, evaporating hope for a swift passage after the historic June 19, 2019, hearing. I don't need a crystal ball to know that absent another George-Floyd-level type of atrocity or massive numbers of Blacks and allies demanding it, the future for passage of a federally chartered reparations commission in the Congressional and/or Executive Branch will be challenging. Thus, I am feeling more buoyed now with the proliferation of local reparations foci, and hope that it lights the fire under the federal effort.

The recommendations subsumed within the California Reparations Task Force Interim Report largely address solutions through basic and necessary public policies that government should be engaged in anyway. This is an area I constantly struggle with. Reparations will unquestionably encompass public policy, but how does one ensure that it is distinct from what government should be doing anyway, that inures to everyone? Indeed, in mid-2021, with the work being done on the Hill around human and structural infrastructure, a news reporter asked me whether reparations should be part of the whole infrastructure bill. My response – "Absolutely not!" "Reparations should not be confused with the needed benefits that's coming from the various infrastructures for proposals," I stated emphatically. "Reparations must be *more* than public policies that benefit society as a whole." Indeed, that's why affirmative action failed to qualify as a form of reparations, as it morphed into programs that benefit virtually all disadvantaged groups. A true reparations settlement must specifically connect the dots back to harms from the enslavement era and its vestiges and living legacies from the Jim Crow/apartheid era down through injustices manifest today.

Finally, I was pleased that the Interim Report took great pains to define its use of words and terms, such as "nigger," "white supremacy," and "unhoused." I was also elated with the use of descriptions such as "freedom-seekers" as opposed to "fugitives" and "enslaved" rather than "slaves." Critical narrative change begins with how language is used, and the Task Force's intentional use of strong activist language is inspiring. I was surprised, however, that the Report was relatively silent on illuminating the definitions of newly invented, albeit controversial, ways of referring to Black people that some activists have sought to promote over the past several years, such as Foundational Black Americans, American Descendants of Slavery, and Freedmen. Perhaps this silence was the result of a lack of consensus amongst Commissioners. Or, strategically, the Report may have been silent on this so that its recommendations would garner more acceptance by the public as opposed to being subject to division. I as well as the Reparations Movement as a whole anxiously look forward to the Task Force's Final Report, and it is my hope that it will close some of the loopholes expressed herein.

Phenomenal. Breathtaking. Groundbreaking. Historic. That was my impression of the December 9–11, 2021, momentous gathering where state and local reparations leaders converged in Evanston, Illinois, for its first national symposium. Hosted by former Alderman Robin Rue Simmons' new FirstRepair organization and convened by the National African American Reparations Commission, the gathering was a powerful potpourri of sharings and learnings, prefaced by a historic tour of Evanston's redlined neighborhoods and topped off with a riveting Town Hall meeting featuring actor–activist Danny Glover and Congresswoman Sheila Jackson Lee.

As moderator of the symposium's Town Hall, I welcomed the audience, both those in person and those viewing virtually across the country and the world, "to this auspicious moment where we bear witness to the beauty of history in the making. A beautiful moment indeed, as we stand on the shoulders of our ancestors, and at the drawing table with our contemporaries, as the concept of reparations is sweeping the country like a storm."

Providing greetings were Robin Rue Simmons and Circuit Court Judge Lionel Jean Baptiste. To ensure that viewers understood the connected continuity of this historic municipal initiative I stated, "Robin Rue Simmons, founder and Executive Director of FirstRepair and former 5th Ward Alderman for the City of Evanston, stood on the shoulders of Judge Lionel Jean Baptiste, who two decades earlier was first elected to Evanston's City Council and the following year, 2002, engineered Evanston's passage of a resolution in support of the federal bill H.R. 40, laying the foundation for an Alderman nearly 20 years later to creatively use tax revenue from the city's legal cannabis industry to fund reparations initiatives."

The Town Hall's panel of seven included labor economist Dr. Julianne Malveaux; Tulsa, Oklahoma, Councilwoman Vanessa Hall Harper; Rev. Dr. Michael Nabors of the NAACP and senior pastor of the historic Second Baptist Church in Evanston; Evanston Alderman Peter Braithwaite; Henry Wilkins, Evanston's Education Reparations Committee Chair; Kamm Howard, National Co-Chair of N'COBRA; and Eric Phillips, Vice Chair of the CARICOM Reparations Commission, who traveled to the U.S. from Guyana as an official representative of CARICOM, the unified community of Caribbean nations. Congresswoman Jackson Lee joined via the big screen, reparations ambassador Danny Glover made poignant remarks, and NAARC convener Ron Daniels made closing remarks, proudly witnessing the fruit of his vision.

As I looked out at the colorful audience, sparse as the result of a cold, rainy, and windy Illinois evening, I felt warm inside. Warm because this was a moment I had been seeking for 50 years, since sitting on that curb and opening the Black Panther Party paper to point number three of its Ten-Point Program. My mind wafted to the various ten-point programs of my cherished Black Power past. Indeed, ten-point programs were always in vogue, even down through NAARC's milestone Ten-Point Program today, which was intentionally modeled after the CARICOM model, which I discuss in Chapter Five. Nostalgia, but then reality clicked in as I resumed my moderator duties for that historic evening, steering the wisdom of the participants.

I had been witness to and presented at the first Evanston Town Hall also featuring Danny Glover, held the same December week two years earlier, all of us unmasked as the COVID-19 pandemic had not yet struck. Despite consternation that mobilization on local levels could forestall movement on the federal level, I stated from the stage that there was no conflict. It was not "either or," but "plus AND." Indeed, the local can inform the national, and vice versa. And that proclamation is coming to pass.

Evanston's choice to use tax revenue from sales emanating from its legal cannabis industry to fund reparation projects in the town was not only genius but also poetic justice as historically, the city's Black population disproportionately comprised the majority of arrests for marijuana offenses. Evanston committed $10 million from its cannabis sales taxes over a ten-year period to seek to address the racial economic wealth gap between Blacks and whites; its first initiative was to provide African American residents with housing assistance and economic development benefits. Erika Alexander expertly documented the twin journeys of former Evanston Alderman Robin Rue Simmons, the architect of Evanston's reparations initiative, and Congresswoman Sheila Jackson Lee, the mover and shaker of H.R. 40, in her illuminating 2022 documentary, *The Big Payback*.

As local jurisdictions seek models, Evanston provides the perfect example, possessing all the ingredients needed to ensure success:

historical documentation and data from the Shorefront Legacy Center, headed up by historian Dino Robinson; an enthusiastic advocate with decision-making authority ready to go the nth mile, in the person of Rue Simmons; a realistic and lucrative revenue source in the form of a tax on cannabis; access to experts on the issue, in the form of the National African American Reparations Commission and Howard University's Thurgood Marshall Civil Rights Center; and the grassroots organizational support of N'COBRA.

Evanston also enjoyed other collaborators during its first years of mobilization, including

- Stakeholders (Black and non-Black communities, faith leaders).

- Legal entities (city corporation counsel, outside counsel, African American Redress Network).

- Government (City Council, City Manager's Office and Staff; Equity and Empowerment Commission, Reparations Subcommittee).

- Local historians (Shorefront Legacy Center, Evanston History Center).

- Financial institutions (banks, credit unions).

- Philanthropy (RSAE Reparations Fund, City Reparations Fund, Evanston Community Foundation, Lewis-Sebring Family Foundation).

- Local reparations organizations (FirstRepair, N'COBRA).

The December 2021 stirring Town Hall was preceded by a high-profile working session. From the moment I entered the room I knew this convening was different. It was the stuff that history books would look back on. The type of primary material researchers would plow through. The nitty-gritty of an auspicious, embryonic burgeoning. The powerful working session was flush with community-based advocates, stakeholders, elected officials, and academic and philanthropic partners working on municipal reparatory justice initiatives. The intimate working sessions provided participants with firsthand information about the background, historical basis, evolution, and process that led to Evanston becoming the first U.S. municipality to award reparations to eligible African American residents, emanating from living legacies of the enslavement era.

"Reparations is a process, not a transaction," trailblazer Rue Simmons emphasized. An important statement, particularly as one considers the danger of a proliferation of hastily thrown together proposals.

The symposium provided the unprecedented opportunity to be part of and help shape ground-breaking momentum. One of my contributions was speaking to the critical importance of narrative change. Rather than succumb to the dominant claim that passage of reparations for Black people constitutes reverse racism, I strongly expressed the need to chart new legal standards. Impressed with the role I consistently saw being played by the National African American Redress Network in assisting municipalities with research and legal counsel, I can confirm there is fertile ground for a coming together of strong legal minds and I and others are playing a role in helping to actualize that.

Cities from Amherst, Asheville, Boston, Chicago, Denver, and Detroit, to Kansas City, Los Angeles, Omaha, Philadelphia, Sacramento, San Francisco, and Tulsa, were all present in Evanston, each reporting on details, strengths, and weaknesses of the organizing efforts in their jurisdictions for reparatory justice.

I loved Keith Young's statement that despite progress "being a battle," that Asheville was "only a few eggs short of making the cake," referring to the necessary components of a city reparations initiative. In an impressive cross-generational presentation between Kansas City organizing veteran Mickey Deen and millennial Will Bowles, it was emphasized that "equity is not enough." That statement, I feel, sets the stage for what I envision to be the next battle amongst reparationists and those merely seeking parity.

Finally, drilling down deeper into local efforts, the convening included presentations by the Bethesda Moses African Cemetery, whose representative, Dr. K. Karen Williams, ardently spoke of land, sacred space, and legacy in the wake of the desecration of Moses Cemetery in Bethesda, Maryland, close to where I reside. "This is the scene of a crime," Williams intensely warned as she hauntingly chanted the conclusion of her presentation. "This is the scene of a crime. Let them lie in peace. They will follow you home in your sleep."

Similarly, descendants of the Chattahoochee Brick Company in Georgia provided a captivating 101 on the issue of convict leasing, enumerating the senseless list of invented crimes through which "slavery continued by another name," such as vagrancy, loitering, and being out after dark. After being convicted and leased to companies such as Chattahoochee, our ancestors were literally worked to death, amassing untold wealth for countless corporate entities still profiting today, such as American Express, Wells Fargo, Wachovia, and more.

NAARC Commissioner V. P. Franklin reported on colleges and universities during the work session, emphasizing the debt students have as they leave college, and Enith Martin Williams focused on her creation of a Reparations Finance Lab. Jurisdictions and organizations at the working sessions had diverse visions and were at different stages of development. All now have a blueprint. These personal renderings represent just a few glimpses from that impressive gathering in Evanston — the first of what will be many to come as reparations continues to blaze across the country.

California and the City of Evanston are great firsts, as they have taken the issue of reparations from a footnote in history to today's center stage. For so long, reparations for Black folk was fringe, relegated to comedic stints, talk show fodder or op-ed space fillers. That has now changed. Although far from perfect, remedies have begun, bit by bit past any naysayers' "but."

The work has begun. The work is far from perfect. The work continues.

UNITED STATES REPARATIONS INITIATIVES CHART SNAPSHOTS

50-State List of Reparations Statements & Laws, January 2020–September 1, 2022 (Including the District of Columbia)	
Alabama	An Alabama House Judiciary Committee panel in April 2021 advanced legislation creating a reparations commission.
Alaska	A bill protecting the cemetery of the indigenous Aleut people was signed into law in April 2021.
Arizona	LOCAL In 2020, a reparation plan from Flagstaff's Black community was presented to the Flagstaff City Council.
Arkansas	NONE
California	In 2021 Governor Newsom signed AB 3121, landmark legislation to establish a first-in-the-nation task force to study and make recommendations on reparations for slavery and its vestiges. In 2022, the California Reparations Task Force issued its Interim Report providing an in-depth overview of harms and a preliminary set of recommendations. A final report is scheduled to be issued in 2023.
	LOCAL Los Angeles Mayor Eric Garcetti, along with mayors of ten other cities in the United States, pledged in 2021 to pay reparations to small groups of Black residents in the city. The mayor announced members to the city's Reparations Task Force. Legislation establishing a Reparations Task Force was passed in San Francisco in 2020. A committee was approved in 2021. Also in 2021, the city established the Dream Keeper Initiative, a $60 million annual commitment to address wealth disparities and social outcomes. The Palm Springs City Council in 2021 issued a formal apology for the city's role in the forced eviction of Black and Mexican families during the 50's and 60's, referring to the devastation as a "city engineered holocaust."

Colorado	NONE
Connecticut	Proposed bill introduced in House Judiciary Committee in 2021 to study "racial inequity and inequality."
Delaware	LOCAL On December 3, 2020, the Wilmington City Council passed a resolution to study reparations.
District of Columbia	A reparations resolution was introduced in the Council of the District of Columbia in 2021.
Florida	NONE since 1994 when the Florida Legislature paid $150,000 to each of the eleven survivors of the 1923 Rosewood Race Massacre and created a scholarship fund for students of color.
Georgia	LOCAL The Athens-Clarke County Commission unanimously passed a resolution in January 2021 calling the government-operated, eminent domain destruction of the Black community of Linnentown an act of white racism and terrorism. The mayor issued an apology for the incident.
Hawaii	No significant findings for Blacks, but natives of Hawaii are still waiting for officials to fulfill the promises of land legislation signed into law in 1995.
Idaho	NONE
Illinois	LOCAL In 2015 the City of Chicago passed a variety of reparatory justice measures to atone for the tortures of its police department. In March 2021, Evanston became the first U.S. city to make reparations available to its Black residents for past discrimination and the lingering effects of slavery. Officials voted to set aside the first $10 million in tax revenue –$25,000 in housing grants for those eligible – from the now-legal sale of recreational marijuana to fund programs that narrow the city's racial wealth gap in order to address the area's history of housing discrimination that affected Black residents, including practices such as redlining.
Indiana	NONE

Iowa	LOCAL The Iowa City Council in September 2021 authorized the Iowa City Truth and Reconciliation Commission as a tool to investigate claims of racism, provide reparations for discriminated-against groups, and do community outreach.
Kansas	LOCAL Two Kansas City Council Members are proposing an ordinance to create a 15-member Mayor's Reparation Commission.
Kentucky	LOCAL In October 2021, Louisville Mayor Greg Fischer signed the city's Metro Council's resolution in support of a study on reparations for descendants of slavery.
Louisiana	NONE
Maine	NONE
Maryland	On February 10, 2020, a bill was introduced in the House of Delegates to study reparations (it was killed in committee). LOCAL In Greenbelt, a suburb of Washington, DC, voters passed a referendum directing the City Council to create a 21-person reparations commission for African Americans and Native Americans in the City of Greenbelt and to make recommendations.
Massachusetts	A Massachusetts State Bill was introduced in January 2021 (notably, it does not reference slavery directly but rather current inequities). LOCAL In Boston, the City Council unanimously approved a resolution in June of 2022 apologizing for the city's role in the trans-Atlantic slave trade and pledging education and the removal of "prominent anti-Black symbols." In Cambridge, a City Policy Order was issued demanding establishment of reparations; it was passed with amendments in September of 2021. In Amherst, the Town Council in June 2021 approved a fund to invest more than $2 million over ten years to help end structural racism and achieve racial equality.

Michigan	LOCAL The Detroit City Council passed a resolution in June 2021 establishing a City Council reparations task force. On August 18, 2020, the Kalamazoo County commissioners moved to create a reparations commission.
Minnesota	LOCAL On January 13, 2021, the St. Paul City Council passed a resolution to study reparations.
Mississippi	NONE
Missouri	LOCAL The St. Louis Board of Aldermen passed legislation in April of 2022 establishing two reparations funds to "support African Americans who have been victims of the effects of slavery" and provide economic development for disinvested neighborhoods. Mayor Tishaura Jones supported and signed the bill.
Montana	NONE
Nebraska	NONE
Nevada	NONE
New Hampshire	NONE
New Jersey	In 2020 the New Jersey State Assembly introduced a proposed reparations task force to conduct research and develop reparatory proposals and recommendations to address generational harms. The bill has not moved out of committee.
New Mexico	NONE
New York	On March 7, 2022, the New York State Assembly passed a bill establishing a commission on reparations remedies; it offers an appropriation of $250,000. The bill will be reintroduced in 2023.
North Carolina	LOCAL The City of Asheville in 2020 decided to apologize for slavery while offering reparations in the form of funding programs aimed at increasing homeownership and business opportunities for Black residents in the mostly white city.
North Dakota	NONE

Ohio	NONE
Oklahoma	LOCAL In June of 2021 the Tulsa City Council passed a resolution to acknowledge and apologize for the continual harm of the 1921 Tulsa Race Massacre. In August 2022 a Tulsa judge allowed a lawsuit based on public nuisance and unjust enrichment to officially move forward. The lawsuit includes as plaintiffs three living survivors who were children at the time of the massacre. In 2001 the Tulsa Race Riot Reconciliation Act provided a scholarship fund and memorial to commemorate the June 1921 race slaughter.
Oregon	A 2021 bill establishing a reparations program is in committee.
Pennsylvania	State Representative Chris Rabb introduced legislation in 2019 that is still in legislative limbo, in committee.
Rhode Island	LOCAL In August 2022, Providence Mayor Jorge O. Elorza signed an Executive Order constituting a formal municipal apology for Black enslavement, urban renewal policies and practices, and acknowledgement of the harms to Black and Indigenous communities. In addition, Mayor Elorza unveiled a budget plan for $10 million allocated for reparations policies.
South Carolina	NONE
South Dakota	NONE (for Blacks, but Native Americans have been offered $1.3 billion for land whites stole from them)
Tennessee	NONE
Texas	NONE
Utah	NONE
Vermont	A 2021 Vermont State House bill examining reparations is stuck in committee.

Virginia	In 2021 the Virginia legislature passed a reparations bill that targets five schools with ties to slavery, including the University of Virginia and the College of William and Mary, all of which owe their foundational success to the forced labor of enslaved human beings who helped build and run the institutions in their early days. LOCAL In Loudoun County, the Board of Supervisors voted in September 2021 to launch a study of the county's history of racism and to seek appropriate remedy.
Washington	LOCAL Seattle's King County Reparations Project
West Virginia	A 2021 state House bill studying and developing reparations is in committee.
Wisconsin	NONE
Wyoming	NONE

CHAPTER FOUR: BONFIRE!

Universities, Corporations, Religious Institutions, Descendant Initiatives:
Opening Up the Caskets

Although much discussion on reparations has been focused on federal, state, and local legislative initiatives, there is growing public focus on other American institutions and entities that benefited from the MAAFA of the trans-Atlantic slave trade and the big business of the criminal enterprise of enslavement in America. Countless companies and industries were enriched because of the enslavement era. There are companies that sold life insurance policies on the lives of enslaved persons, such as Aetna, New York Life, and AIG. Gains were made by financial giants J.P. Morgan Chase, Manhattan Bank, Fleet Boston Financial Group, and Bank of America. Others with documented ties to slavery include railroads Norfolk Southern, CSX, Union Pacific, and Canadian National. Newspaper publishers that assisted in the capture of runaway slaves included Knight Ridder, Tribune, E.W. Scripps, and Gannett. The financial backers of many of the country's top universities, including just about every Ivy League university, were wealthy enslavers.

So, the internal work a few of these institutions are doing is promising, if not yet promissory.

Amongst the most poignant to me is the February 2021 pro-reparations essay written by Matthew McCarthy, the CEO of Ben & Jerry's Ice Cream. "Corporate America has a special role to play in encouraging our nation to address this history," McCarthy wrote for *Fast Company* and the October 2020 report by the American

Sustainable Business Council, called "Creating an Economic System that Works for All." Many of these leading players across America have had internal discussions but, outside of some prominent student protests at certain universities – with the notable exception of the February 2021 Harvard Medical School Lancet Commission on Reparations and Redistributive Justice, which showed that reparations would have helped Black people in America survive COVID with a much more equal playing field – there has largely been a lack of visible, external discussion about how those establishments benefited whites at the expense of Blacks.

Ben & Jerry's, however, is not the only corporate entity calling for a reckoning with the past. Amalgamated Bank in March 2021 became the first major U.S. bank to endorse H.R. 40. There are, however, countless companies and industries that benefited and were enriched from the profits made because of chattel slavery.

Deadria Farmer-Paellmann wants the Bank of America, amongst many others, to pay. The founder and Executive Director of the Restitution Study Group, an idea formed in 2000 to secure reparations and restitution from corporations complicit in the antebellum enslavement of Africans, she has been on a long and lonely campaign to get Bank of America to admit to being complicit in the slave trade back when it was the Providence Bank of Rhode Island. That bank turned its head and put blinders on its revenues from custom duties, fees, and tariffs for slave ships. "While this alone is egregious enough, the matter is worse due to the fact that the slave traders were trading in violation of Rhode Island and the United States laws prohibiting the slave trade," Farmer-Paellmann wrote in a letter to Bank of America. Therefore, she has said, Bank of America should cough up those back fines, for each enslaved African and for each slave ship, and have it all put into a trust for Black people.

It is beyond fitting that a woman of African descent is challenging a bank named after America. But she is not the only one forcing American institutions to look at themselves. Think tanks and advocacy groups now see reparations as a social justice issue and have made it part of their platforms. The bodies of George Floyd, Breonna Taylor, Trayvon Martin, and others definitely played a role, but this internal wrangling has happened only because activists have never stopped publicly explaining, teaching, and arguing about the true nature of American history and how American capitalism has exacerbated the abuses of African descendants, Indigenous peoples, Asians, Latinx, and even poor whites. For decades reparations advocates have challenged corporations that benefited from the profits made from the trafficking in human beings during the enslavement era. They are now being listened to and understood. And after the racial turmoil exposed since 2020, more are trying to hear.

An often-overlooked group of companies benefitting from Black suffering were those that provided mass communications. Media 2070, a project of Free Press, a media advocacy and watchdog group, produced a 100-page essay examining the history of anti-Black harm in the U.S. media system and is in the forefront of illuminating this issue. From the critical role that trafficking of enslaved Africans played in making this country's earliest newspapers financially viable, to decades of the targeting of Black press and journalists, the history of harm runs deep. An example: newspaper publishers such as Knight Ridder, Tribune, E.W. Scripps, and Gannett assisted in the capture of runaway persons and, after enslavement, newspapers frequently published prejudicial and inflammatory stories causing false information to spread like wildfire, intensifying white mob vehemence and violence. This mass communications dynamic is then traced to the present day, when deregulation has resulted in very few Black owners of traditional media – while racist algorithms amplify the voices of white supremacists across online platforms like Facebook, Twitter, and YouTube.

Says the summary by Media 2070, "Media organizations were complicit in the slave trade and profited off of chattel slavery; a powerful newspaper publisher helped lead the deadly overthrow of a local government in Wilmington, North Carolina, where Black people held power throughout the city; racist journalism has led to countless lynchings; Southern broadcast stations aired vociferous opposition to integration; and, in the 21st century, powerful social-media and tech companies are allowing white supremacists to use their platforms to organize, fundraise, recruit and spread violent hate."

Media 2070's goals include the following:

- Black people have the social and financial resources needed to tell our own stories from ideation to distribution – and this truth has helped facilitate parallel truths in various Indigenous communities and other communities of color.

- Community members transform media systems and infrastructure toward becoming reparative.

- An abundance of media showcases the possibilities of repair and reconciliation.

- Students are learn about how the media have harmed communities and created racial injustice. Students also engage with possibilities for change.

- Media reparations is an accepted common-sense concept.

- Media-reparations legislative/litigation wins exist.

- Reparations legislation at local, state, and federal levels includes media-specific language.

- Media reparations is an issue intersectionally woven into various movements for economic justice, racial justice, and human rights.

- Deeper solidarity exists between media-justice organizers/activists and organizers/activists who find political homes in allied movements.

Notice the impact the Reparations Movement has had. The Media 2070 reparations project lists acknowledgement of harm and specific redress and even wants media to be added to the local efforts. And the mainstream media has taken notice in the last two years: the *Boston Globe*, the *Baltimore Sun*, and the *Hartford Courant* have issued front-page apologies for the role they perpetuated during the enslavement era, including everything from inflammatory racist language to slave advertisements.

The Western university, for many years, has been an almost-forgotten beneficiary of the enslavement era. Amongst the financial backers of many of the country's top universities were wealthy slave owners. Some universities have decided to publicly acknowledge it and a small number have committed to action. Georgetown University, which stands today because of the sale of Black people owned by its founding Jesuits, has announced $100 million toward descendants of 272 persons who were sacrificed to keep the university from going into bankruptcy. Harvard has followed suit, with an announced $100 million reparations fund in 2022 and a promise to find the descendants of the campus' enslaved persons.

There is also serious collective work. The organization Universities Studying Slavery has sponsored several meetings. The consortium consists of more than 95 universities and colleges in the United

States, Canada, and the UK. "Member schools are all committed to research, acknowledgment, and atonement regarding institutional ties to the slave trade, to enslavement on campus or abroad, and to enduring racism in school history and practice," as quoted from its documents. The group was created by the University of Virginia President's Commission on Slavery and the University "to ensure that UVA's important work would spread beyond Virginia and to respond to the calls for guidance from other schools."

Indeed, the University of Virginia has a blasphemy right in its own state that cries out for research, acknowledgement, and atonement. When a representative of the descendants of the Richmond, Virginia, Howlett family reached out to me last year with his ancestral story of 264 acres of land stripped from them after the enslavement era, I was livid. Not only is it now the site of the exclusive Willow Oaks Country Club, but what's more, a lucrative granite quarry was subsequently discovered within the stolen land, and its precious stones were used to build the Old Executive Office Building on the grounds of the White House in Washington DC, as well as the Navy and War Department buildings in the Nation's Capital, as well as the capitol building in Richmond.

Meanwhile, on campuses across the country, statues of enslavers are tumbling down, alternative campus tours are offered that emphasize the university's slave history, and students are organizing for divesture of endowments that are stained with the blood of the slave trade.

The American church is not standing still, either. I was honored to participate in a mid-July 2021 press conference designed to push Congress to pass H.R. 40 before it left on August break. The July 13th presser – an event co-sponsored by a myriad of America's faith communities, including the National Council of Churches, the United Church of Christ, and the Religious Action Center of

Reform Judaism, along with advocacy organizations – was held at the United Methodist Building in Washington, DC. Rev. Aundreia Alexander, then Associate General Secretary of the National Council of Churches, was instrumental in pulling this gathering of faith leaders together.

There to both bear witness and, as Jim Winkler, President and General Secretary of the National Council of Churches, said, to "turn up the heat" on a hot summer day, we stood in a sacred circle to show that we were unified in our goal of putting pressure on Capitol Hill. "Our ancestors are our priority, from Juneteenth to the deaths caused by the health disparities of COVID-19," I declared from the podium, representing NAARC. So many religious leaders there had waited so long for this moment, as Mary J. Novak, then newly-named Executive Director of the NETWORK Lobby for Catholic Social Justice, explained – in her case, 32 years. The "selfishness" and "collective soul sickness" displayed by white nationalists and racists during their January 6 terrorist insurrection, Novak declared, "nee[d] to be countered with the Gilad balm to heal one of America's central sins."

As I stood there listening, surrounded by a true rainbow of inter-racial religious activism, I appreciated the extent of the growth that has taken place in America since Black Power activist James Forman delivered his 1969 manifesto demanding that white synagogues and churches pay Black people reparations for their role in the trans-Atlantic slave trade and the maintenance of slavery and Jim Crow. Bishop Eugene Sutton of the Episcopal Diocese of Maryland (which voted in 2020 to create a $1 million seed fund for Black programs in Baltimore and beyond) also addressed the presser: "We [in the diocese] began to ask ourselves, what does justice require?" To hear this was exhilarating. Predominately white religious institutions have gone from ignoring the issue to asking the right questions.

Another effort very close to my heart, based on my Black Nationalist underpinnings, is that of land. As instilled in me by the teachings of Malcolm X and the New Afrikan Independence Movement, "land is the key to freedom, independence, and self-determination." That is a primary reason why the return of Bruce's Beach in Manhattan Beach, California, to the descendants of its original African American owners in June 2022 resonated so much to me and was a turning point in the advocacy of descendant communities for redress.

Willa and Charles Bruce bought the land in 1912 for $1,225. They created a beach resort for Black residents, who had few desegregated California coast options. They built a bath house, dance hall, and café. As a result, they inspired other Black families to purchase adjacent land. The goal was to have an oceanfront retreat. But the resort quickly became a target of white supremacy – attacks, vandalism, and a 1920 confrontation with the Ku Klux Klan. The Bruces tried to stand tall, but the City of Los Angeles stepped in and did what the Klan could not: it moved to condemn their property and the surrounding areas in 1924, seizing it via eminent domain. The resort closed and the Black landowners lost their land as the Depression hit in 1929. The Bruces sued and tried again with no result while the proposed park the city had used as an excuse to take the land didn't happen until 1960 – and was only constructed to prevent more lawsuits from the Black victims. The land went to the state, then to LA County. This madness finally stopped in June 2022, when the Los Angeles County Board of Supervisors voted unanimously to transfer the land to Marcus and Derrick Bruce, Charles and Willa Bruce's great-grandsons. The family agreed to lease the land back to the county for a whopping $413,000 a year. The settlement also contains clauses allowing the Bruces to later sell the land to the county for a price of up to $20 million.

Acknowledgement of wrongdoing. Redress. Compensation. This is a pivotal story, not only because what was stolen is being returned, but also because it's a public acknowledgement of wrongdoing – it makes historic discrimination real, and current. Countless atrocities have been buried, narratives silenced, and history, essentially, rewritten. This is the kind of story that reparations advocates cannot repeat enough, and kudos to millennial activist Kavon Ward, now director of the organization Where is My Land? for bringing this victory to fruition.

We must carry on the clarion call of Mamie Till-Mobley, the mother of 14-year-old Emmett Till. She courageously demanded an open casket so the public could see the brutalization of her son for themselves, making sure that no longer would the blood, sweat, and tears of our forebears be erased.

Indeed, caskets are being thrust open across the country, uncovering more and more evidence of historical racial atrocities, lynchings, and massacres. Past damages are being exposed and redressed, seemingly daily. There are current efforts for redress from Ocoee, Florida's 1920 Election Day bloodbath and the 1919 terrorism that ravaged the Elaine, Arkansas, Black community. The land housing the unimaginable horrors of Atlanta's Chattahoochee Brick Company, which continued slavery in the name of convict leasing, is being reclaimed by the people. Recommendations from the 2000 Race Riot Commission investigating the 1898 racial insurrection and coup d'état in Wilmington, North Carolina, are waiting to be passed by the legislature. In 2019 remnants were discovered from the slave ship *Clotilda*, which in 1860 illegally transported Africans to Mobile Bay, Alabama, more than 50 years after the international slave trade was abolished, and descendants today are talking about amends.

Descendant advocacy initiatives are taking the proverbial bull by the horns seeking repair as their visibility has surged in the wake of media coverage of Bruce's Beach. Pastor Rev. Dale Snyder of Bethel AME Church in Pittsburgh, whose rich history dates to the Underground Railroad, has been aggressively organizing to return ownership of the church's appropriated land and be awarded development rights. For more than 100 years the church had essentially become the surrounding Black community's epicenter: its hospital, daycare, and school – all of which were obliterated in 1957 when the church property was seized by eminent domain and demolished.

Northeastern University's Civil Rights and Restorative Justice Project and its Legacy Coalition under the leadership of former Judge Margaret Burnham seeks to secure reparative justice for American citizens whose ancestors were lynched in acts of racial terror during the Jim Crow era. Similar to the efforts of Northeastern University is the African American Redress Network, a union between Howard University School of Law's Thurgood Marshall Civil Rights Center and Columbia University. This collaborative entity supports engagements at the grassroots, regional, and state levels in promoting racial justice for specific instances of U.S. historical wrongdoings by undertaking and facilitating multidisciplinary research, capacity-building, education, and legal advocacy.

There are also strong advocacy movements in Maryland, including the Bethesda African Cemetery Coalition (BACC), led by Dr. Marsha Coleman Adebayo, and the Lakeland Community Heritage Project in Greenbelt, piloted by Rev. Dr. JoAnne Braxton of the Braxton Institute. BACC is fighting to block the continued desecration of an ancestral cemetery. Lakeland is determined to gain reparations through and from the City of College Park and the University of Maryland in restorative and transformative justice strategies. And in New York, there are those seeking amends for the loss of intergenerational wealth as the result of the displacement of Black New Yorkers in the 1800s from Seneca Village, a neighborhood in

Upper Manhattan demolished for the city to build the sprawling Central Park.

The goal of the Justice for Greenwood Foundation in Tulsa, Oklahoma, has been to secure respect, reparations, and repair for the Greenwood Community for the 1921 Tulsa Race Massacre and to provide direct services and support of survivors and descendants, public education, and legal and policy advocacy. The massacre left as many as 300 Black people dead and 40 square blocks of exclusively Black businesses, homes, and schools obliterated. Attorney Damario Solomon Simmons and his legal team won a victory in August 2022 when a court allowed a lawsuit with three living survivors of the massacre to proceed against the city.

Tracy McCurty's Black Belt Justice Center has focused on a campaign by Black farmers to rectify injustices stemming from the Black farmers' 1999 class action racial discrimination lawsuit against the U.S. Department of Agriculture for land justice for decades of government-sanctioned racial discrimination in the delivery of loans and farm subsidies to Black farmers. The goal of the 1999 lawsuit was to restore Black farmers and their agricultural land base through full debt cancellation, federal and state tax relief, monetary damages for economic harm, priority of services, and access to land.

These examples represent a mere microcosm of illicit and immoral acts perpetrated by both private individuals and public officials against descendants of Africans enslaved in the U.S., which have left in their aftermath Black people and once-thriving communities uprooted, terrorized, traumatized, and scarred – physically, mentally, and economically – generationally. They represent a mere tip of the iceberg; there are countless other hidden caskets yet to be exhumed. As the whirlwind of change sweeps the country, the Reparations Movement is engaged in history in the making, scarily wobbling at the tipping point of triumph or collapse. What happens next will not only cultivate and chronicle critical narratives, but also possibly portend the future of democracy, both domestic and global.

✳ CHAPTER FIVE: COMBUSTION!

**International Appeals for U.S. Basic Human Rights;
CARICOM Points the Path for Global Reparations**

Blacks have historically appealed to international bodies for the vindication of basic human rights. But it was Queen Mother Audley Moore, President Imari Obadele, Chokwe Lumumba, and others who lit the fire under me to study the topic further, long before I entered law school. Throughout the 20th century, Queen Mother Moore ensured that the issue of reparations would be front and center, building upon advocacy as part of her Ethiopian Women's Organization, which petitioned the UN in 1957 on behalf of Black people for self-determination and against genocide, and in 1959 for land and reparations. She was also the first signee of the Provisional Government of the Republic of New Afrika's Declaration of Independence at its founding convention in 1968, which included the issue of reparations as one of its central tenets. Queen Mother Moore was also a founding member of N'COBRA, and I was blessed to have her, as well as Rosa Parks, cradle my newborn baby girl in their arms at the 1994 N'COBRA convention in Detroit where they were both being honored. But it was Queen Mother's persistence on the issues of genocide and reparations, along with those of Obadele and Lumumba, that led me to delve deep into international human rights during the 1970s.

Gracing my bookshelf for years before I truly recognized its value and impact was the 1970 book *We Charge Genocide* by the Civil Rights Congress and edited by William Patterson, based on the 1951 petition *We Charge Genocide: the Historic Petition to the United Nations for Relief from a Crime of the United States Government Against the Negro People.* W.E.B. Du Bois, William Patterson, Mary McLeod Bethune, Paul Robeson, Mary Church Terrell, and George Crockett were amongst nearly 100 signees of the appeal for redress which chronicled the genocidal sufferings, murder, mental assault, and crimes against humanity inflicted against Black people. Curiously, Queen Mother Moore's name is absent amongst the signees, despite the fact that she was the most prolific contemporary of the day on the issue of human rights and reparations. Perhaps, and probably, she was considered too radical for the times. Indeed, reparations is not mentioned in the Petition. Perhaps she demanded it be included and was denied. Perhaps, for some other reason, she was ostracized. Perhaps, as a woman, she was considered too outspoken. I anxiously await the publication of the upcoming scholarly book chronicling the life of this prolific warrior woman by Professor Ashley Farmer. Perhaps blanks will be filled in.

The Petition upon which the 1970 book was based on was presented in 1951, three years after the UN General Assembly adopted the International Convention on the Prevention and Punishment of the Crime of Genocide (Genocide Convention). That Convention confirmed that "genocide, whether committed in time of peace or in time of war, is a crime under international law which the Contracting Parties undertake to prevent and punish." Genocide, the Convention declares, is the committing of certain acts "with intent to destroy, in whole or in part, a national, ethnical, racial or religious group."

According to the international convention, the following acts constitute genocide:

- killing members of the group
- causing serious bodily or mental harm to members of the group

- deliberately inflicting on the group conditions of life calculated to bring about its destruction in whole or in part

- taking measures to prevent births within the group

- transferring children from one group to the other

Pursuant to the Genocide Convention, genocide is not the only punishable act. Related acts, such as conspiracy, incitement or attempts to commit genocide, and complicity in genocide, are equally punishable. Furthermore, the international definition concludes by reminding the Parties that those who commit genocide or any other of the related acts "shall be punished, whether they are constitutionally responsible rulers, public officials, or private individuals."

When the *We Charge Genocide* historic petition was presented to the UN in 1951, the United States had yet to ratify the Genocide Convention. Indeed, it took 38 long years for the U.S. Senate to give its advice and consent to ratification. Outrageously, one of the articulated reasons for this unconscionable delay was the fear that Blacks in America would use the treaty to their advantage, which is exactly what the 1951 Petition sought to do. In 1987, however, political leaders in the U.S. felt comfortable that enactment of anti-segregation laws mooted concern over attacks against American racial practices of the 1950s and 1960s. Nevertheless, upon ratification, the Senate took the extra step of inserting language to limit the scope of the Convention within U.S. law. On April 4, 1988, President Ronald Reagan signed the Genocide Convention Implementation Act, which codified the international Genocide Convention in U.S. law, making minor changes in an attempt to limit its application in U.S. law. For a more robust discussion of the issue and process, see my white paper "Racism in the U.S. Criminal Justice System: Institutionalized Genocide," published by the American Constitution Society for Law and Policy.

Curiously, it is unbeknownst to most in this country that the international Genocide Convention has been part of U.S. law since 1988. There should be no reason why that law, or any of the laws pursuant to the New International Law Regime that surfaced during the early 1960s, should not be zealously used in U.S. courts to support claims for Black people. One example that I was personally involved with was the July 6, 1988, opinion issued by Judge Charles Haight of the U.S. District Court for the Southern District of New York in response to a motion to dismiss a criminal indictment on prisoner of war grounds in the case of Mutulu Shakur, filed by Attorney Chokwe Lumumba and myself, with Lennox Hinds of the International Association of Democratic Lawyers as amicus. The judge required the U.S. Attorney to respond to our motion, and they thereupon assembled a team of five lawyers from the Departments of State, Army, and Defense. Our motion argued that the Geneva Convention of 1949 and its 1977 Protocols on armed conflict and the treatment of prisoners of war should be applicable to Mutulu Shakur. The judge scrutinized our arguments, the government's hostile rebuff of them, and, as expected, denied relief. We later demanded release of Black political prisoners and prisoners of war as a down payment on a reparations settlement with the United States. This request was not as far-fetched as one might have deemed, as one of the provisos from the Japanese American reparations bill was a pardon for all those convicted of resisting detention camp incarceration. There is precedent. The government has authorized it before. They can do it again.

Since the 1951 Genocide Petition and in the absence of genuine opportunities for redress within the U.S. body politic, Black people in the U.S. have made constant appeals to international bodies for vindication of their basic human rights. We have made conscious and consistent attempts to internationalize our plight as we struggle to both effect changes in the country's priorities, policies, and practices, as well as assert our right to self-determination. I have already addressed the 1957 and 1959 efforts of Queen Mother Moore.

In 1971 RNA President Obadele addressed a letter to the member nations of the UN General Assembly, directly following a pre-dawn unprovoked attack by U.S. governmental and state police forces upon his residence and the office of the Provisional Government of the RNA, requesting that international observers be sent to Mississippi and "act immediately to avoid loss of life and a conflagration and in the interests of world peace."

In 1978 the Provisional Government of the Republic of New Afrika submitted a letter to Salim Ahmed Salim, Ambassador of the United Republic of Tanzania to the U.N. and Chair of the UN Special Committee of 24 on Decolonization. The missive requested international help for Black prisoners of war and independence, releasing the names of 17 people whom the RNA stated were not just political prisoners but prisoners of war within the meaning of the Geneva Convention of 1949 and its 1977 protocols. The letter emphasized that the "U.S. government has never accorded the status of POW to a single Black, Puerto Rican or Indian engaged in liberation struggles against the U.S.," and that the U.S. was in violation of UN General Assembly Resolutions 2621 and 3103 with respect to the treatment of combatants captured in the course of struggles against colonial and alien domination and racist regimes, and in violation of Article 5 of the Geneva Convention of 1949 which guarantees that all persons claiming POW status will be granted that status until a decision by a competent tribunal. The final ask was that the UN Special Committee of 24 facilitate the exchange of New Afrikan prisoners of war from the U.S. to Cuba.

In 1979 Attorney Lennox Hinds filed a petition with the UN on behalf of three petitioning organizations: the National Conference of Black Lawyers, the National Alliance Against Racist and Political Repression, and the United Church of Christ's Commission for Racial Justice. This same petition was filed with the UN Human Rights Commission and its sub-commission on Prevention of Discrimination and Protection of Minorities. Here the petitioners alleged a pattern of gross violations of human rights and fundamental freedoms of political prisoners and prisoners of war wrongfully held on account of their race, economic status, and political beliefs and inhumanely treated in U.S. prisons.

Inspired by the U.S. ratification of the Genocide Petition which had been submitted to the UN 46 years earlier, the National Black United Front in 1997 delivered a petition containing 157,000 names of people who again formally charged the U.S. government with genocide against its Black population.

In 2006, the Inter-American Commission on Human Rights accepted my request through the Justice Roundtable coalition, which I convened, to hold a thematic hearing on the 100:1 quantity disparity between crack and powder cocaine as the most egregious example of mandatory minimum sentencing in the U.S. criminal punishment system. The petition argued that de facto discrimination against African Americans that is a result of harsh mandatory minimum sentences for crack cocaine cases is a violation of the American Declaration on the Rights and Duties of Man – specifically the right to equal protection under the law, the right to a fair trial, and the right to judicial protection against violations of fundamental rights. Professor Charles Ogletree delivered the Roundtable's testimony, joined by the first UN Independent Expert on Minority Issues Gay McDougall; directly impacted person Kemba Smith; and the Honorable Patricia Wald. Wald, a former judge of the International Criminal Tribunal for the former Yugoslavia, testified on behalf of the American Bar Association, and poignantly testified:

Unduly long and punitive sentences are counter-productive, and candidly, many of our mandatory minimums approach the cruel and unusual level as compared to other countries – as well as to our own past practices. On a personal note, let me say that on the Yugoslavia War Crimes Tribunal, I was saddened to see that the sentences imposed on war crimes perpetrators responsible for the deaths and suffering of hundreds of innocent civilians often did not come near those imposed in my own country for dealing in a few bags of illegal drugs. These are genuine human rights concerns that I believe merit your interest and attention.

In 2014 after the horrific police killing of Michael Brown in Ferguson, Missouri, Attorney Justin Hansford led the "Ferguson to Geneva" delegation, accompanying Ferguson protestors and Michael Brown's parents to testify before the UN Committee Against Torture. "We need the world to know what's going on in Ferguson and we need justice," said Leslie McSpadden, the mother of Brown, as she testified in Geneva, Switzerland, eerily echoing Mamie Till-Mobley's heartfelt choice for an open casket for the world to see what racism did to her son.

For several decades more than 110 African American and Latino men and women were subjected to torture that was racially motivated and included electric shocks, mock executions, suffocation, and beatings by John Burge, a Chicago police commander, and his subordinates. Scores of Chicago police torture survivors suffered from the psychological effects of the torture they endured, and for redress they appealed to the international arena. A shadow report on the Burge torture cases was submitted to the UN Committee Against Torture. In May 2006 and November 2014, the UN Committee condemned the U.S. Government and the City of Chicago for failing to fulfill their obligations under the Convention Against Torture concerning the Burge torture cases. The Committee also cited its concerns about police militarization, racial profiling, and reports of police brutality. The international body's intervention was pivotal to the May 2015 passage by the Chicago City Council of a Reparations Ordinance providing compensation, restitution, and rehabilitation to survivors of the racially motivated police torture. The Ordinance contained a formal apology to the survivors, a Commission to administer financial compensation, free enrollment in city colleges to the survivors, the requirement that the city's public schools teach about the torture, and the funding of city memorials about the torture.

In November 2014, We Charge Genocide (WCG), a Chicago-based grassroots inter-generational organization whose name was inspired by the historic UN 1951 Petition on Genocide, sent a delegation of eight youth to the 53rd Session of the UN Committee Against Torture in Geneva to present evidence of police violence. The delegation was following up on the submission of a shadow report, "Police Violence Against Youth of Color," published by WCG. The goal of addressing the UN was to increase the visibility of police violence in Chicago and call out the continued impunity of police officers who abuse, harass, and kill youth of color in Chicago every year.

On September 24, 2019, the Inter-American Commission on Human Rights convened a thematic hearing on reparations as a remedy for human rights violations against Afro-descendants in the U.S. during the 173rd Period of Sessions, spurred by the Thurgood Marshall Civil Rights Center at Howard University School of Law, along with 29 co-sponsoring organizations. The international hearing, which I had the honor of testifying before, highlighted the need for reparations for the systematic pattern of human rights violations against Afro-descendants attributable to the U.S. government, including the crimes of slavery, Jim Crow laws, excessive and violent policing practices, mass incarceration, and other forms of structural racial discrimination.

On June 17, 2020, an "Urgent Debate" in the UN Human Rights Council in Geneva was convened, focused on systemic racism and policing in the U.S. The session followed demands for international action issued by human rights groups and experts from dozens of countries who cited the repeated deaths in the U.S. of unarmed Black people, brutal police tactics against protestors, and police assaults on journalists covering the protests. A letter filed by the U.S. Human Rights Network and endorsed by family members of George Floyd, Breonna Taylor, Michael Brown, and Philando Castile called on the Council to pass a resolution that would have established an independent international commission of inquiry related to the systemic racism, human rights violations, and other abuses against people of African descent in the U.S. and around the world. The resolution was not adopted but a weaker version was passed which failed to mandate the establishment of such a commission. Instead, it called for a report from the High Commissioner to be presented to the Human Rights Council, followed by an interactive dialogue.

As part of the Urgent Debate on Racism and Police Brutality held at the UN Human Rights Council in Geneva, UN High Commissioner for Human Rights Michelle Bachelet called on countries to examine their pasts and to strive to better understand the scope of continuing "systemic discrimination." She pointed to the "gratuitous brutality" on display in the killing of George Floyd, who had died in Minneapolis on May 25 after a white police officer, since convicted with murder, kneeled on his neck for nearly nine minutes. She also stressed the need to "make amends for centuries of violence and discrimination, including through formal apologies, truth-telling processes and reparations in various forms."

In October 2021, upon request by the Spirit of Mandela organization, I served as Chief People's Counsel in New York before an International Tribunal of jurists, charging the U.S. government with violations of international human rights, on behalf of Black, Brown, and Indigenous People residing in the United States. In prosecuting the case I used the definition of genocide as a lens in scrutinizing five key issue areas – policing, mass incarceration, political prisoners, environmental racism, and public health system inequities – and their impact on Black, Brown, and Indigenous communities. The international jurists returned a verdict of guilty, and the Spirit of Mandela organization is using the verdict in its educational activities throughout the country.

There has been a continuous evolution of appeal by people of African descent in the U.S. to the international sphere for recognition and redress, and these recitations merely scratch the surface. The evidence and documentation presented to these international bodies clearly reveal patterns and practices of gross violations of human rights and fundamental freedoms in the U.S., which should lead to reparations. And the UN has been listening. In June 2021, four months before the Spirit of Mandela International Tribunal, UN Human Rights Chief Bachelet issued a report that called for the defense of all African people against police brutality. Its conclusion encompasses four elements: "We need to step up, pursue justice, listen up and redress." *Reparations on Fire* is devoted to all four.

The fire for reparations has not been contained to the continental United States. As all activists have learned, the Caribbean – our mini-Africa away from Africa – historically can be either a very conservative place or a very radical place. When I think of the Caribbean, I think of great Blacks such as Maroon leader Queen Nanny, the Honorable Marcus Garvey, poet Claude McKay, historian C.L.R. James, the legendary Bob Marley, revolutionary leader Maurice Bishop, and author Walter Rodney. And now, as I smile from ear to ear, I must include the first President of the new republic of Barbados, Dame Sandra Mason. The fact that these individuals all come from different islands is less important to me than the fact that together their fingers have the potential to form a mighty fist, which they have started with the formation of CARICOM – the political and economic union of 20 Caribbean countries working together to help shape policies for the region and achieve collective goals.

The CARICOM Reparations Commission (CRC), established in 2013, is a shining example of a concise plan of action for reparatory justice. Its Ten-Point Action Plan delineates the path for reparations for the victims of enslavement in the Caribbean and their descendants. With a mandate to "prepare the case for reparatory justice for the region's Indigenous and African descendant communities who are the victims of Crimes Against Humanity in the forms of genocide, slavery, slave trading and racial apartheid," the CRC has engaged the United Kingdom and other former colonial European nations on the importance of redress.

The CARICOM Reparations Commission is chaired by University of the West Indies Vice Chancellor Professor Sir Hilary Beckles, author of a momentous book which graces my bookshelf, *Britain's Black Debt: Reparations for Caribbean Slavery and Native Genocide*. In addition to the national and regional CRC governing bodies, some Caribbean nations have their own commissions. In the island of Grenada, once the center of the struggle of Maurice Bishop, its local Chair, Arley Gill, echoed the sentiment of the CRC as he spoke words encompassing the necessary importance of apology as a first step in establishing the moral, ethical, and legal case for the payment of reparations. "I believe we must demand that the descendants of those who profited from slavery must acknowledge the harms inflicted upon enslaved Africans and their descendants," he declared in a statement marking Grenada's Emancipation Day. Although it's been 184 years since England abolished slavery, the 400-year damage has resulted in "unimaginable brutality, unthinkable cruelty and gross injustice meted out against our ancestors . . . we should never let our ability to resist and rise above these grave injustices stand in the way of fighting for what we know is right and just." Gill concluded by emphasizing the importance to African humanity of a "sincere apology from European nations, the Catholic Church, and associated corporations . . . to finally correct a wrong that has lingered in our history and our collective memory for too long."

Meanwhile, in the same month of August 2022, a Reparations and Racial Healing Summit was convened in Accra. The Ghanian nation's President, Nana Akufo-Addo, took the spotlight to call for reparations for slavery for the African continent, the diaspora, and the Caribbean.

Earlier that year, England's royal family got quite a surprise when they toured their former colonies. William and Kate, the Duke and Duchess of Cambridge, heard harsh words from the streets of the Bahamas and Jamaica. It got so bad that Prince Edward and Sophie, the Earl and Countess of Wessex, postponed their Grenada trip because they heard angry calls for reparations from Antigua and Barbuda, Saint Vincent and the Grenadines, and Saint Lucia. I guess by now the royals have learned that the African Reparations Movement in the UK has been leading calls for compensation for decades. That movement grew when it was revealed by HM Treasury, the British government's finance ministry, that British taxpayers had been paying off the "so-called debt," to white enslavers who, like their white American enslaver counterparts, were compensated over their loss of "property" when the slave trade was abolished. Outrageously, the payments to the white descendants of slaveholding families in the UK continued until 2015! Diane Abott and David Lammy, two prominent Black Members of Parliament, have backed reparations calls.

While digesting these appalling facts three things came to mind. First, I reflected how in 2021 Germany agreed to pay its former colony, the African nation Namibia, $1.2 billion in reparations because of a 1904–1908 genocide enacted against Africans there. Then I considered how serious the UN was getting: during the summer of 2021, in reaction to the George Floyd and Breonna Taylor protests around the world the previous year, it called for a study of how police interact with those of African descent around the world. I then turned to the seriousness of the requests from the Caribbean to pursue reparations from the Western world.

Calls and efforts for reparations in the Caribbean have taken form in collective regional efforts as well as initiatives on the country level, such as in Jamaica. It wasn't surprising that Jamaica – the home of the legendary Maroons who escaped slavery and took to the nation's hills – took the lead, demanding compensation from Britain from the 17th and 18th century trans-Atlantic slave trade. According to the National Library of Jamaica, an estimated 600,000 Africans were shipped to Jamaica for enslavement. First colonized by Spain and then Britain, Jamaica was a British colony until it became independent in 1962. In this international time of racial reckoning, its citizens wanted reparation for damages experienced by their African ancestors, forcibly removed from their homes for forced labor that benefited the British Empire, as a form of justice. The cost: U.S. $10 billion.

The white-supremacist debt owed to Blacks in America is similar to that owed the Caribbean by Britain and other European colonizing countries for the genocide of the Native population and subjecting Africans to slavery after forcing them from Africa to the Caribbean as slaves and later laborers. There is another similarity: when the United States abolished slavery in 1865, it paid reparations to white slave owners, the same way Britain paid reparations to its slaveholders when it formally abolished slavery in 1834 and the same way the new Republic of Haiti, the 19th century Black Power nation of the Caribbean, was mandated, as a condition of recognition of its freedom, to pay reparations to the French it had defeated to achieve independence.

As America was reacting in 2021 to the half-billion-dollar donations of MacKenzie Scott to the nation's HBCUs, UK philanthropist Bridget Freeman the same year gave a half-million-dollar donation in the name of reparations to the University of the West Indies. CARICOM Chair Sir Hilary Beckles said in a press release: "Bridget has accepted her responsibility and willingness to be held accountable. In this regard, she is a reparations hero, and we hope that the millions of other British citizens in her position will step up, come forward, and participate in the healing and development that is reparations." Although, I submit, the donation should not be counted as reparations, I see it as an important step.

Professor Chinweizu of Nigeria, author of *The West and the Rest of Us*, noted in a 1993 major address at the second Plenary Session of the First Pan-African Conference on Reparations in Abuja:

> We must acknowledge that we are not the only people in the world who are seeking or who have sought, reparations. In fact, by only now generating a mass movement in pressing our claim for reparations, we are latecomers. I will not at this time catalogue the precedents for reparations, paid and pending. I will just suffice it to say that with such precedents for reparations to non-Black peoples spanning four continents, it would be sheer racism for the world to discountenance reparations claims from the Black World. But our own search for reparations must, of necessity, be tailored to our own peculiar experience. Some others may need only that their ancestral home range be returned to them; some others that acts of genocide and other atrocities against their people be atoned for and paid for; some others that lands excised from their territory be paid for. We, however, who have experienced all of the above and more, and

experienced them for much longer than most, and therefore suffer chronically from their effects – we must take a more comprehensive view of what reparations must mean for us. We must ask not only that reparations be made for specific acts, we who have been such monumental victims are obliged to also ask, what sorts of systems, and policies and practices, made this long holocaust possible? And what must be done to transform these systems and policies and practices such that such injustice will never be so inflicted again?

The mandate of the CARICOM Reparations Commission is to prepare the case for reparatory justice for the region's Indigenous and African descendant populations who were the victims of crimes against humanity through genocide, slavery, the slave trade, and racial apartheid. CARICOM recognizes the special role and status of European governments in these crimes and developed specific assertions and a Ten-Point Action Plan for reparatory justice.

The CARICOM Reparations Commission asserts that European governments:

- Were owners and traders of enslaved Africans and instructed genocidal actions upon Indigenous communities

- Created the legal, financial, and fiscal policies necessary for the enslavement of Africans

- Defined and enforced African enslavement and Native genocide as in their "national interests"

- Refused compensation to the enslaved with the ending of their enslavement

- Compensated slave owners at emancipation for the loss of legal property rights in enslaved Africans

- Imposed a further one hundred years of racial apartheid upon the emancipated

- Imposed for another one hundred years policies designed to perpetuate suffering upon the emancipated and survivors of genocide

- And have refused to acknowledge such crimes or to compensate victims and their descendants

CARICOM's Ten-Point Plan requires:

1. Full Formal Apology

2. Repatriation

3. Indigenous Peoples Development Program

4. Cultural Institutions

5. Public Health Crisis

6. Illiteracy Eradication

7. African Knowledge Program

8. Psychological Rehabilitation

9. Technology Transfer

10. Debt Cancellation

Across the Atlantic, the 2015 formation of the National African American Reparations Commission, convened by the Institute of the Black World 21st Century, was specifically inspired by CARICOM, and its Ten Point Program is similar to CARICOM's plan.

The points of the NAARC platform are:

1. Apology & Maafa Institute: A Formal Apology and Establishment of an African Holocaust (Maafa) Institute

2. Repatriation: The Right of Repatriation and Creation of an African Knowledge Program

3. Land: The Right to Land for Social and Economic Development

4. Funds: Funds for Cooperative Enterprises and Socially Responsible Entrepreneurial Development

5. Health & Wellness: Resources for the Health, Wellness, and Healing of Black Families and Communities

6. Education: Education for Community Development and Empowerment

7. Housing & Wealth Generation: Affordable Housing for Healthy Black Communities and Wealth Generation

8. Info & Comms Infrastructure: Strengthening Black America's Information and Communications Infrastructure

9. Sacred Sites & Monuments: Preserving Black Sacred Sites and Monuments

10. Criminal Justice System: Repairing the Damages of the "Criminal Injustice System"

CARICOM's plan for reparatory justice is also analogous to N'COBRA's five injury areas developed as part of its Litigation Strategy Commission which met over the course of a number of years at Howard University School of Law. The five injury areas encompass (1) peoplehood/nationhood, (2) education, (3) health, (4) criminal punishment, and (5) wealth/poverty.

Amidst my unfaltering praise, my only critique of CARICOM's reparations platform is its tendency to not describe African enslavement as genocide. CARICOM is far from alone in this. Why is it that the term genocide is recognizable for Native peoples but not African descendants under enslavement, particularly since we now have an international definition that goes far beyond yesteryear's perception of the term genocide being limited to mass killings?

Moreover, I'm frustrated when I hear advocates parrot international law and standards, attempting to pigeonhole our claims within rubrics advanced by the experiences of oppressed peoples in other countries. Indeed, I'm arguably guilty of such practices as well – e.g., my constant voice, as just mentioned, uplifting the global definition of genocide as applicable to Black people in the U.S. But when such rubrics limit claims, because they fail to take our historical realities into account and thereby fail to serve our purpose, should we use them as the standard, or develop our own criteria and influence their adoption by the world community?

For example:

While it is apropos that we uplift the UN General Assembly's December 2005 "Basic Principles and Guidelines on the Right to a Remedy and Reparation for Victims of Gross Violations of International Human Rights Law and Serious Violations of International Humanitarian Law," which outlines the forms of reparation as including restitution, compensation, rehabilitation, satisfaction, and guarantees of non-repetition, the instrument nevertheless fails to expressly include within its ambit of the term "victim" the generational realities of the international capturing and chattelization of human beings. As such, can there ever be "full" reparations for the descendants of Africans enslaved in North America? Indeed, the concept of "full reparations" referred to in international law is unrooted in the reality of a crime against humanity that goes far beyond economically assessable harms, lost opportunities, and material damages.

NAARC's Preamble expressly states that "no amount of material resources or monetary compensation can ever be sufficient restitution for the spiritual, mental, cultural, and physical damages inflicted on Africans by centuries of the MAAFA, the holocaust of enslavement and the institution of chattel slavery." Thus, a more fitting nomenclature is beginning to gain traction, that of "comprehensive" reparations. This concept, advanced through collective discussion relative to the unique situation of descendants of Africans in the U.S. and subsumed within a document prepared by the National Black Cultural Information Trust (NBCIT), defines comprehensive reparations as systems that make reparatory justice accessible and inclusive, and that focus on repairing harms endured by people of African descent and their communities, as the result of the systems of chattel enslavement and Jim Crow/U.S. apartheid, and all their continuing vestiges and living legacies resulting in modern-day systemic racism, and the repair of injured communities. As illuminated by Jessica Ann Mitchell Aiwuyor in NBCIT's document "Understanding Comprehensive Reparations":

> Comprehensive reparations recognize that each period of harm cannot be disconnected when seeking to repair injuries on a large scale. . . . Some reparations advocates focus only on the period of chattel slavery. However, this limitation does not sufficiently account for ongoing harms, the continuation of enslavement under different names, and the ongoing vestiges of slavery.
>
> Comprehensive reparations prioritize accessibility and reject false and invasive purity ancestry standards for

large-scale reparative justice initiatives and redirect focus on documented harms to communities. Lineage-based reparations are under-inclusive, create costly barriers and are too restrictive for large-scale local governments, state, and national reparative justice initiatives. Eliminating unnecessary barriers to access is essential for reaching and repairing Black communities. Comprehensive reparations focus on repairing harms and not punishing Black communities for lack of slavery documentation by focusing on continual injuries for historical accuracy and accessibility. Comprehensive reparations include African Americans and descendants of Africans harmed by the vestiges of slavery in the U.S, regardless of national origin. Comprehensive reparations uplift DAEUS [descendants of Africans enslaved in the United States] and descendants of free or maroon Black communities and people of African descent residing in the United States that were also harmed by the vestiges of slavery and Jim Crow, regardless of national origin. All are owed forms of reparative justice.

Finally, comprehensive reparations can also include direct family-based repair, providing remedies to descendants of harmed persons in specific families or neighborhoods. Since this often requires different and complex types of verification, this is best utilized for smaller-scale family-based reparative justice initiatives, such as the GU-272, Bruce's Beach, Tulsa Race Massacre survivors, etc. In these cases, the descendants of harmed families and groups can be directly remedied by at-fault parties on a case-by-case basis, at a smaller scale that prioritizes accessibility.

So, what does all this recent past mean to the present and future? Simply this: African people all over the world are on fire, waking up to the reality of a real, practical move toward true justice. The collective "We" are beginning to understand that we are one people who went through the same particular experience, a special trauma committed by another group of people and their instrumentalities. The descendants of that group are in power today because of that experience. As such, a long-overdue reckoning on race is being called for throughout the diaspora, in the words of Malcolm X – "in this day, at this time, which we intend to bring into existence, by any means necessary"!

✿ CHAPTER SIX: WILDFIRE!

My Miscellaneous Musings on Reparations

I'm going to be quite honest. Prior to 2020, I had not given a whole lot of thought to a vision as to what reparations can look like because most of my life's work as part of the Reparations Movement since age 16 has been to convince people not to be scared of the word and concept. Indeed, for 99 percent of the past five decades, although engaged in activism and advocacy around reparations, I have essentially, albeit unknowingly, been planting seeds for the moment we are in now – where the Movement and societal conditions have ripened to seriously discuss, deliberate, and debate the who, what, when, and how of effectuating a viable reparations package. This is the excitingly historic time of visioning, the time our ancestors have been waiting for.

Reparations is broad, deep, and filled with nuance and interpretation. As such, there are a myriad of views and ideas as to what the concept can entail for Black people. I might agree with some views and disagree with others. My personal views, or anyone else's for that matter, should not be rubberstamped as the standard for the Reparations Movement. Rather, all views should be part of the necessary national dialogue pursuant to a federally chartered commission that studies and develops reparation proposals, considers all evidence, and determines what it will take to create a viable reparations package. Gathering the best minds in the country is important, but we also need the views of the sisters and brothers on the street corner, elderly Black women in church hats, and Black entrepreneurs, among others.

It's important and pertinent that the views of everyone are listened to and considered, unencumbered by media and undue sensationalism.

At my core are the words of the revolutionary martyr Amilcar Cabral: "Always bear in mind that the people are not fighting for ideas, for the things in anyone's head. They are fighting to win material benefits, to live better and in peace, to see their lives go forward, to guarantee the future of their children." The ordinary, average, everyday person on the street is not necessarily interested in the grandiose ideas in the minds of the elite, but in how these concepts are going to impact them in their everyday daily lives, such as, *How are we going to get the potholes fixed?* and *What about these young men dealing drugs on the street corners?* That's what was in the mind of Mississippi Mayor (the elder) Chokwe Lumumba, a former leader of the Republic of New Afrika, when confronted in post-election real life, as opposed to his status as a revolutionary activist. "We might have our grandiose ideas," he said, "but it also is important to find out what the masses are thinking, what they feel about this issue." Bottom line: it is important all the way around to find out what the victims, the injured parties, feel about reparations.

Too often the average person is excluded from discussions, resulting in the creation of mere symbolic change. Simply naming a building after an enslaved Black person or offering scholarships devoid of consultation with injured descendants and communities is not the way in which a reparations settlement should occur. For example, at one point I was part of the legal team of one of the family groups descended from the people sold by the Jesuits to save Georgetown University from bankruptcy. I was surprised to hear some family members say, "We just want our ancestors' graves to be kept up."

They weren't talking about simply putting a name on a building. They were talking about resources in a way that was impactful to them. They wanted the upkeep of graves as an area of redress. Thus, it is critical that the injured parties themselves have a very key role in determining just what reparations for them should look like and include.

I've gone against the current political grain by proclaiming that reparations is more than a closing of the Black/white wealth gap. Indeed, I take exception to the highly promoted idea that reparations is primarily about that. My mantra, as I stated before, is "the harms of the enslavement era and its vestiges were multifaceted; thus, the remedy must be multifaceted as well." There are mass incarceration issues, health disparity issues, issues involving educational inequities. There is psychological damage. In sum, reparations is about repair; about closing and remedying gaps – the mental, psychological, cultural, psychological, educational and justice injuries. The remedies must be as multifaceted as the harms.

I get the very practical need for cash payments. My mentor Dr. Imari Obadele would often not so very jokingly say, "I need resources to get my teeth fixed." I think that there's value in letting people decide how they might want to use resources. That's when dealing with cash resources makes a lot of sense. However, I have frequently expressed that a reparations settlement must entail more than money. In the early days, we talked about cash as the chief form of redress. Today, my analysis has matured beyond that. As Professor Chinweizu of Nigeria, author of *The West and the Rest of Us*, noted in 1993 in his major address at the second Plenary Session of the First Pan-African conference on Reparations in Abuja, "Reparatory justice is not just about money. It is not even mostly about money. In fact, money is not even one percent of what reparatory justice is all about. Reparation is mostly about making repairs: mental repairs, psychological repairs, cultural repairs, organizational repairs, social repairs, institutional repairs, technological repairs, economic repairs, political repairs, educational repairs, health repairs."

A reparations settlement can be fashioned in as many forms as necessary to equitably address the many forms of injury sustained from chattel slavery and its continuing vestiges. Such forms can include cash payments, land, educational scholarships, tax relief, community development, historical monuments and museums, pardon of political prisoners, repatriation resources, as well as the elimination of laws and practices that maintain dual systems in major areas of life, including the criminal punishment system, health, education, and the financial economic system. Many of these points are subsumed within both the NAARC Ten-Point Program and N'COBRA's five injury areas for redress.

It's pertinent to understand that reparations is not solely an economic concept, but a political and cultural one as well. It's not limited to just stolen labor, but is also for unjust war and cultural aggression. The political essence of slavery is not founded merely in the exploitation of labor, but also in the illegal imposition of U.S. jurisdiction on the enslaved and their descendants. It really can never be overemphasized that Black people are on this soil as the result of vicious kidnapping, cultural and physical rape, economic exploitation, child slavery, mental bondage, and terror. The full ramifications of this historical record must not be endlessly ignored.

Let us not forget about the freedom of Black revolutionaries who were the victims of the COINTELPRO era. When the United States granted reparations to Japanese Americans, one important provision was a pardon for all those who resisted being put in those World War II detention camps. There are Black political prisoners and prisoners of war in this country who resisted the war that the United States has been waging against Black people in many different forms. One of those forms was the COINTELPRO, the Federal Bureau of Investigation's illegal counter-intelligence program whose mission was to disrupt and destroy the Black movement. The tactics resulted in the mass incarceration of Black radicals from the late 1960s to the early 1980s. Many of these individuals are still in prison today, while others are in exile, and still others have been released subject to limiting parole restrictions. They should all be pardoned, along with posthumous (after-death) pardons for Marcus Garvey, Callie House, Imari Obadele, and more.

People often query why the federal government should be responsible for reparations; they ask, *Wasn't all the injury done by the states?* I credit my response from the teachings of my mentor, Brother Imari Obadele, father of the modern-era Reparations Movement. He often schooled me that we must remember the origins of the Black Nation in the United States. We are the descendants of Africans kidnapped and transported to the U.S. with the explicit complicity of the U.S. government and every arm of the U.S. lawmaking and law enforcement machinery: U.S. federal law, state law, high court decisions, lower court decisions. The dehumanization, atrocities, and terrorism of our enslavement in the U.S. were not isolated occurrences but a matter of war – one conducted under the specific authority of the United States Constitution. Brother Imari constantly preached that the kidnapping was a wrongful act for which our ancestors and we as their heirs are entitled to damages. The enslavement was an equally wrongful act for which our ancestors and we as their heirs are entitled to damages. The stealing of our labor was a wrongful act, as was the genocide we are still suffering. We are entitled to damages – to reparations, to reparatory justice, he drilled into me. The compensations we speak of are owed to us.

Article One, Clause One, Section Nine of the United States Constitution expressly guaranteed and sanctioned the importation of kidnapped African prisoners of war to every state that might desire us until the year 1808. That article also upheld the further dehumanization of the African by relegating our status to that of three-fifths of a white person. And most egregious, it was a war conducted against the African on this soil under the authority of yet another constitutional provision: Article Four, Section Two, Clause Three, also known as the Fugitive Slave provision, which mandated that no enslaved person, even if he or she had reached a free state, was safe, and it was the duty, the legal obligation, the constitutional responsibility of every white man, woman or child to track down the escaped African and deliver him or her up to the U.S. government. Reparations now!

The 13th Amendment, passed in 1865, recognized the freedom of all enslaved Africans and made it illegal to continue slavery in the U.S. (except for that ridiculous "except as punishment for crime" clause). No payment, however, was made to Black people for anything. In fact, the Dred Scott case had been decided scarcely eight years prior in which a Supreme Court Justice ruled that a Black person in America "had no rights which a white man was bound to respect" and that neither Dred Scott nor any other Black person could be a citizen of the U.S. in the manner in which that word was used in the Constitution.

The burden of proving historic injury should not be an individual task, with the country denying the reality that whole groups have been harmed to the degree where each person within the group is automatically injured. There must be acknowledgment and remedy as a matter of reparatory justice for the continuing, pervasive, genocidal damage that initiated with the founding of this country.

Who among Black people should receive reparations? I don't make a distinction. This might put me at odds with other pro-reparations activists. People ask hypothetically, "Well, should Oprah get a check?" Hell, yeah! I say that because reparations are damages for injury or harm. If Oprah goes out in the street and a car hits her, when she goes to court, she's entitled to damages. It's a legal principle. Now, what she decides to do with those damages is her business. I would hope that Oprah and her fellow Black billionaire Robert Johnson, the founder of Black Entertainment Television, and other highly resourced Black folk would do honorable things with their reparatory resources, but I would not say that because someone has a certain amount of wealth that they're not entitled to this remedy.

I don't make distinctions because I understand from a personal standpoint the precariousness of our financial situation. Black people don't have wealth; they have the same buying power as others but have less money in the bank. I'm no exception. I live in a pretty good neighborhood. I have a nice house, but it took a hell of a lot to get where I am right now. I've had to work for a living because I had no capital gains to live off. Indeed, my financial status is nowhere near the status of my comparable white lawyer colleagues who are the beneficiaries of intergenerational wealth. I don't have that. And equity, while critical, is not sufficient. Reparations is the missing element.

If Oprah or Bob asked for my advice, I would tell them to consider putting their reparations resources into repairing the five injury areas we as N'COBRA founders outlined decades ago – education, wealth, health, peoplehood, and the justice system. I would also list each of the ten areas recommended as part of the NAARC Ten-Point Program for consideration – apology, repatriation, land, economic development, health and wellness, education, housing and wealth, information and communications, sacred sites and monuments, and the justice system.

Reparations, reparatory justice, restitution, restorative justice. There are questions surrounding these seemingly simple demands. Are they all synonymous? What are the distinctions? What is the difference between reparations and general public policy? There is much dialogue, deliberation, and debate. People are looking for guidance. The time for simple but effective definitions has arrived.

Because the movement for reparations is escalating at breakneck speed, it's really hard for me to envision exactly what this centuries-long quest for justice can and should look like in the next several years. Again, that's the beauty of establishing a federally chartered Reparations Commission. The vision must be part of a deliberate process where people come together to decide – discuss and debate back and forth, in town halls, listening sessions, and other forums. With such a collaborative process, I'm confident that the most brilliant suggestions will arise.

It is the height of pomposity for one person or one organization to pronounce what the reparations solution will be, and demand acceptance without the benefit of what is called "African consensus." Until we sit in a room together as civil human beings and seriously begin to work this out, we're not going to be able to see through to the future.

I'm thrilled that Hollywood is paying attention to reparations because that means the topic is part of the national consciousness. Erika Alexander's documentary *The Big Payback* chronicles the journeys of Robin Rue Simmons, architect of Evanston, Illinois', successful reparations ordinance, and Congresswoman Sheila Jackson Lee, mover and shaker behind the federal H.R. 40. I have yet to see all the episodes of HBO's critically acclaimed *Watchmen* starring Oscar-winning actress Regina King, but I know that reparations is part of that story's backdrop. The series *Atlanta*, starring Donald Glover, has been creative in episodes centered on reparations. People are clearly dreaming about this, testing out ideas in fantasy. I've never had the leisure to be able to dream about what reparations could look like because that reality seemed so far into the future. Now, the reparations future is not a flying car–type fantasy but a current event, unfolding daily.

Only closing the Black/white wealth gap is not going to remedy the trauma that Black folk have endured or result in the freedom of a former Black Panther who has been in prison for 50 years.

We are history in the making, and that history is equal parts edgy, exciting, transformational, confrontational, messy, and confusing. We are beyond rhetoric now and well into action mode, and I couldn't be happier. These times are exciting. I'm glad I'm still around to be a part of it, to have more than an historic dream, inherited from not only my enslaved ancestors and our collective ancestors from the Motherland, but also those whose feet I sat at, who imbued me with the healing spirit of reparatory justice. Fire can either destroy or purify. The work being done now will either create or destroy the dreams of those of African descent today and in the coming future.

APPENDIX

On September 11, 1987, Chokwe Lumumba, Imari Abubakari Obadele, and myself were invited by the National Conference of Black Lawyers to present at its Race and the Constitution convening at Harvard Law School. Also invited was economist Richard America (yes, that was his name!), who joined us three "independentistas" on the panel.

The discussion addressed the question as to whether a constitutional amendment was necessary in order for Black people in America to achieve reparations. The joint conclusion from the three of us was a resounding "no," because the 13th Amendment already established the basis for definitive action. Brothers Imari, Chokwe, and myself each presented on an aspect of our position at the conference. Obadele subsequently compiled our presentations in a small book entitled, *Reparations Yes! The Legal and Political Reasons Why New Afrikans – Black People in the United States – Should be Paid Now for the Enslavement of Our Ancestors and for War Against Us After Slavery.* As the only living co-author of this historic document, I am proud to include this primary source here.

Note: The *Reparations Yes* text is reprinted exactly as published in 1987. Obadele uses the lower case "i" and capitalizes the "W" in We, to demonstrate that the community is more important than the individual. The words Africa and African, and Pan-Africa and Pan-African are generally spelled as Afrika/Afrikans and Pan-Afrikan/Pan-Afrikans in the original text, and reprinted as such, here. The spellings reflect the words' historical use as part of the New Afrikan Independence Movement. The following explanation comes from *A Brief History of the New Afrikan Prison Struggle*, by Sundiata Acoli:

We of the New Afrikan Independence Movement spell "Afrikan" with a "k" because Afrikan linguists originally used "k" to indicate the "c" sound in the English language. We use the term "New Afrikan," instead of Black, to define ourselves as an Afrikan people who have been forcibly transplanted to a new land and formed into a "new Afrikan nation" in North America.

REPARATIONS YES!

The Legal and Political Reasons Why New Afrikans - Black People in the United States - Should Be Paid Now For the Enslavement Of Our Ancestors And For War Against Us *After* Slavery

ARTICLES BY

CHOKWE LUMUMBA,
IMARI ABUBAKARAI OBADLELE &
NKECHI TAIFA

These articles originally served as the basis for a presentation made to the reparations workshop of the Conference on Race and The Constitution sponsored by the National Conference of Black Lawyers [NCBL], in September 1987, at the Harvard Law School. They are reproduced here with the permission of the authors and with gratitude to the NCBL for creating the occasion.

Dedicated to Sundiata Acoli, Tarik Haskins, Herman Bell, Albert Nuh Washington, Jalil Muntaqim, Masai Ehehosi, Dhoruba Bin Wahad, Kubwa Obadele, Ramona Africa, Imari Obadele Two, Mutulu Shakur, Leonard Peltier, and all the brothers and sisters of our struggle who are soldiers, and the fallen White Anti-Imperialists who have supported us, held much too long in United States jails as common criminals because the United States refuses to acknowledge the legitimacy of our struggle for land and independence.

House of Songhay
COMMISSION FOR POSITIVE EDUCATION
Baton Rouge, Louisiana

TABLE OF CONTENTS

Reparations and Self-Determination
by Nkechi Taifa

Notes on Reparations for New Afrikans in America
by Chokwe Lumumba

Proposed Reparation Amendment
by Chokwe Lumumba

Reparations Yes!
by Imari Abubakari Obadele

A Proposed Act
by Imari Obadele & Chokwe Lumumba

The Japanese Reparations Act
(not included herein)

The Conyers Reparations Study Bill
(not included herein)

The Index
(not included herein)

REPARATIONS AND SELF-DETERMINATION

By Nkechi Taifa, Esq.

The concept of reparations for Afrikans born in North America is not novel, nor is the demand for such compensation new. The concept did not begin with the government of the Republic of New Afrika or the New Afrikan People's Organization. It did not begin with the Afrikan National Reparations Organization, nor did it originate with Queen Mother Moore, Elijah Muhammad, William Patterson or Marcus Garvey. It did not begin with the white American campaign promise of forty acres, fifty dollars and a mule, a promise, like most campaign promises made to Black people, which was never honored. Reparations is a well-established principle of international law, which has been recognized and practiced by the United States.

> The New Afrikan Declaration of Independence states, in part:
>
> *We claim no rights from the United States, other than those rights belonging to oppressed people anywhere in the world, and these include the right to damages - reparations, due us for the grievous injuries sustained by ourselves and our ancestors by reason of United States lawlessness...*

Reparations are a well-established principle of international law. Those who feel this is just another way of begging for "handouts" from the United States government must remember the origins of the New Afrikan nation in North

America. We are the descendants of Afrikans illegally kidnapped and transported here by whites with the explicit complicity of the United States government and every arm of the United States law-making and law-enforcing machinery. We are entitled to reparations. The compensations we speak of are owed to us. Article One, Section Nine of the United States Constitution expressly guaranteed and sanctioned the warfare which constituted the slave trade in Afrikans in every state that might desire it, for twenty years. We need to remember that the United States upheld within its Constitution at Article One, Section Two, Clause Three, the further dehumanization of the Afrikan, by relegating his/ her status to that of three-fifths of a white man. We should never forget Article Four, Section Two, Clause Three – known as the fugitive slave provision. This article mandated that no person held as a slave, even if he or she had reached a "free" state, was safe, and it was the obligation of any party to capture and return him or her, to slavery. We are entitled to damages—to reparations. The compensations We speak of are owed to us.

The principle of reparations is well established. Usually it involves payment from one nation to another for war damages. A classic modern example is the payment of nearly a billion dollars in reparations in the post-World War II era by the Federal Republic of Germany to the state of Israel for the murder of six million Jews in Europe from 1935-1945. (It is interesting to note that at the time of the Jewish atrocities, the state of Israel, which subsequently received the reparations, did not exist). The United States has played prominent official roles in other reparations settlements.

1. WWI - An Allied Reparations Commission supported by the United States, fixed the sum of reparations

to be paid by the defeated Germany at 132 billion gold marks. (The U.S. acknowledged its "right" to German reparations but accepted no reparations). Subsequently the United States, acknowledging and deeply involved in the principle of reparations, achieved an alteration of reparations payment arrangements with the 1924 Dawes Plan, the 1928 Young Plan and Herbert Hoover's 1931 Moratorium.

2. WWII - U.S. Presidents Franklin Roosevelt and Harry Truman worked out the WWII reparations claims formula against Germany and Japan at the wartime Yalta and Potsdam conferences of Allied leaders in 1945. These conferences also assessed reparations against the smaller Axis Powers, Bulgaria, Finland, Hungary, Italy, and Rumania.

3. The U.S. has paid reparations to various indigenous nations and groups in this country for damages and frauds committed against them by U.S. citizens, the several states and the United States, up to 1946, through the Indian Claims Commission.

Notably, there exist recent precedents inside the U.S. for reparations, principally for Japanese-Americans. San Francisco Mayor Diane Feinstein in 1983 signed a bill approving compensation for former Japanese-American employees of the city in the amount of $1,250 for every year they were interned in "relocation centers" set up by the U.S. government during WWII. In 1984, Mayor Tom Bradley of Los Angeles signed a resolution publicly apologizing to city employees who were forced to resign and sent to internment camps. The City Council gave each of them $5000 as a token of reparation. On September 17, 1987 the U.S. House of Representatives passed H.R. 442, a bill granting reparations to Japanese survivors who were placed in concentration camps by the U.S. government during World War II. In addition to $20,000 in reparations, the bill offers a formal apology from the U.S. government.

It is a sad commentary on this country that neither the U.S. government nor any U.S. company has had the dignity to offer even a token of reparation to New Afrikans. Even the argument that affirmative action programs sufficed as reparations settlements would fail, as these programs constantly come under angry attack in reverse discrimination suits brought by primarily white males who resent any type of "special treatment" accorded to classes of people who historically have been forced to take a rear sear to white male advancement.

We as a nation of people are not and have not been respected by the United States of America and, thus, our international law rights have remained ignored. We are not treated as other nationalities who have been wronged. There have been no efforts made to compensate us as has been the case with certain others. Is it because We have, for the most part, unquestionably accepted the "Alice in Wonderland" version of "citizenship" in this country? Is it because We have become complacent as the *best-dressed slaves in the world*? Is it because We persist in acting through a colonized frame of reference, thinking through the mind of the white American, looking through the eyes of white American, hearing through the ears of the white American? Is it because collectively We have been remiss in vigorously analyzing and applying international law precepts to our struggle here in North America?

The concept of reparations is closely aligned to that of self-determination and should not be divorced from it. To complement the demand for reparations, therefore, We must be clear in our quest for self-determination and the knowledge that the various international covenants and resolutions affirming that all peoples have the right to self-determination apply also to New Afrikan people in North America. See Article One of the International Covenant on Civil and Political Rights, U.N. General Assembly Resolution 1514 (XV) 14 Dec. 1960, U.N. General Assembly Resolution 1303 (XXVIII) 12 Dec. 1973.

The Thirteenth Amendment to the United States Constitution is the most direct U.S. law basis recognizing the right of self-determination for Afrikan people in North America. Although we have all been familiar with the phrase, "the 13th Amendment freed you, and the 14th Amendment made you a citizen," how often has it been that We really sat down and analyzed the significance of these historical events? The effect of the 13th Amendment, passed in December 1865, upon Afrikan people in North America should not be underestimated. For, it rekindles questions unsettled since the time of the U.S. Civil War. The effect of this amendment was to eradicate the municipal law which legalized slavery, recognizing the freedom of all held as slaves in this country. This amendment imposed no political conditions whatsoever on the newly freed Afrikan, and contained no statement of citizenship or any other limiting status (aside from the prison slavery clause) in the American community. It has only two sections, whose words are matchlessly simple:

Section One: Neither slavery nor involuntary servitude, except as punishment for crime whereof the party shall have been duly convicted, shall exist within the United States or any place subject to their jurisdiction.

Section Two: Congress shall have power to enforce this article by appropriate legislation.

Interestingly, the U.S. Congress debated the issue of the role of Black people in American society and pointedly did not offer U.S. citizenship to the now-free Afrikan through the 13th Amendment; it simply elevated the status of the Afrikan in the eyes of the white nation to humans, as opposed to mere chattel. Thus, after the 13th Amendment, the relations between the New Afrikan nation and the North American Nation were no longer subject to the unilateral rulings of one political body but, rather, to the regulation of the law of nations.

This principle was established in *United States v. Libellants and Claimants of the Schooner Amistad*, 15 Peters 517, 595-596. In that case, the U.S. Supreme Court addressed the question of Afrikans who had been freed (they had freed themselves) from illegal slavery by Spanish subjects. The Court found that the Afrikans so freed were subject neither to the law of Spain nor to U.S. law but, to "the general law of nations."

If the relevant portion of the 13th Amendment is undisputed, and thus far it is, no one, not even the ex-slave owner of the now free Afrikan could define the future status of the Afrikans for them, and impose a status upon them. This right was the Afrikan's alone, fruit of the right to self-determination.

Thus, because We were a free people, whose independent status was now recognized by the United States, the New Afrikan nation was possessed of rights - irrespective of action or inaction by the American community - and natural questions began to flow. *How do we wish to govern ourselves, should we leave or stay here, what does this freedom mean???* Well, this freedom in today's terminology - the right to self-determination - would extend to us four natural options, *choices*, as to a political destiny: (1) the right to return to Afrika, as we were the victims of warfare and illegal kidnapping; (2) the right to emigrate to another place, as our families were cruelly fragmented and scattered throughout the diaspora; (3) the right to seek admission, as citizens, into the American community and strive for a multi-racial democracy, and (4) the right to remain where We were, negotiate with the native people of this land, and establish our nation in an independent separate territory; for, We had been legally constructed outside the American community and found ourselves on soil claimed by the United States in great numbers and severed homeland ties.

For two and one-half years, in varying degrees, each of these options was exercised by various sectors of the New Afrikan nation. But at no time, however, was a national plebiscite (people's vote) held to inform Black people of these options and permit them collectively to make a choice.

The American community paused, rather than act immediately. They paused for five years before passing a constitutional amendment, attempting to bring the Afrikan inside of the American community. They waited, and left Blacks completely out of their system - left us under the shield of international law, left us with the inalienable right to self-determination.

Thus the 14th Amendment, passed nearly three years after the 13th Amendment and five years after the Emancipation Proclamation could not—as popular interpretation suggests— impose U.S. citizenship upon or grant U.S. citizenship to the newly freed persons. The 14th Amendment (all persons born or naturalized in the United States and subject to the jurisdiction thereof are citizens of the United States and of the state wherein they reside), can only be construed as a proper and necessary *offer* of U.S. citizenship to freed slaves and their descendants, an offer subject to acceptance or rejection. Therefore, once freed by the 13th Amendment, Blacks could not be incorporated into the U.S. body politic without the informed, freely expressed consent of the people.

Regardless of how one interprets the 14th Amendment's citizenship clause, between the time of the first Confiscation Act of 1861 (which prevented the return of persons who had escaped from slavery and reached Union Army lines, or who had been captured by the Union Army) and the 14th Amendment in 1868, was a span of seven years. One can never forget the infamous ruling of U.S. Supreme Court Justice Taney in the Dred Scott case, 60 U.S. 690 (1857), that a Black person in America "had no rights which the white man was bound to respect," and that neither Dred Scott nor any other Black person could be a citizen of the United States "in the manner in which that word was used in the Constitution."

What, then, was the citizenship of freed slaves? The defense in the Amistad case, supra, speaking of Afrikans who had freed themselves on shipboard before falling into U.S. custody, argued as follows:

The domicile of origin prevails until the party not only acquired another but has manifested ... an intention of abandoning his former domicile, and acquiring another as his sole domicile. As it is the will or intention of the party which alone determines what is the real place of domicile which he has chosen, it follows that a former domicile is not abandoned by residence in another if that residence be not voluntarily chosen. Those who are in exile, or in prison, as they are never presumed to have abandoned all hope of return, retain their former domicile. That these victims of fraud and piracy ... never intended to abandon the land of their nativity, nor had lost all hope of recovering it sufficiently appears from the facts on this record. Amistad, 10 L. Ed. at 842.

Clearly, the freed Afrikan, in an analogous position to the Amistad Afrikans, were not U.S. citizens; they would seem to have been citizens of their place of "former domicile" in Afrika. But of which Afrikan nation? Slavery had gone on in North America from 1619 into 1865. By 1600 the social practice and laws of the emerging European nation made it clear that Afrikans, free and slave, were not permitted to join the new white nation, nor were the Afrikans to be allowed to join the "Indian" nations on these shores in peace and in numbers. Thus, a new Afrikan nation evolved in the Western Hemisphere. It was new, because we were becoming a new people, snatched from every region in Afrika, molded by our common history of oppression and struggle into a new nation, a New *Afrikan* nation in the world.

Although cognizant of the white ethnocentric manner in which history is generally framed in the United States, it is pertinent that we begin to untrack our minds and analyze history from an independent frame of reference. We must keep uppermost in our minds our unresolved rights under the 13th Amendment and international law: above all our right to self-determination, with full information, to choose and fashion our own political destiny.

It follows, then, that if the freed Afrikan's right to self-determination was real, the American citizen, who had grown rich from the Afrikan's body and labor and misery had the duty to restore riches to the ex-slaves and their progeny, to "repair" them for the damage they had suffered.

Now, how does this issue of self-determination have a relationship to the demand for reparations today? Simple. The necessary corollary to self-determination is that there must exist the capacity for putting the self-determination process into effect. If the self-determining decision is to accept the U.S. offer of citizenship in the United States, then that citizenship must be unconditional and carry with it the requisite affirmative measures needed to effectively integrate the Afrikan into American society. If the self-determining decision is to return to a country in Afrika, those persons must have transportation resources plus those additional reparations necessary to restore enough of the Afrikan personality for the individual to have a reasonable chance of success in reintegrating into Afrikan society in the motherland. If the self-determining decision is to emigrate to a country outside of Afrika, the person must have the same reparations as persons emigrating to countries inside Afrika. If, finally, the decision is for an independent New Afrikan nation-state on this soil, then the reparations must be those agreed upon between the United States government and the New Afrikan government. The reparations must be at least sufficient to assure the new nation a reasonable chance of success in solving the problems imposed upon us by the Americans in our status as a colonized people.

When history is examined from an independent frame of reference, it is unnecessary to seek a congressional amendment to effectuate the demand for reparations. All that needs to be done is to put the already existing 13th Amendment into effect. The mechanism for effectuating reparations in that amendment lies in its Section Two: "Congress shall have power to enforce this article by appropriate legislation."

In 1972 the Anti-Depression Program of the Republic of New Afrika was submitted to and approved by the National Black Political Assembly Convention meeting in Gary, Indiana. In that same year it was also accepted by the Mississippi Loyalist Delegation to the Democratic National Convention and submitted to various Congresspersons at the Democratic National Convention in Miami, Florida. The Second Act of this Anti-Depression Program was an act authorizing the payment of a sum of money (three hundred billion dollars at that time), in reparations for slavery and unjust war against the New Afrikan nation, and an act authorizing negotiations between a commission of the United States and a commission of the Republic of New Afrika to determine kind, dates and other details of paying reparations. This act represents an example, albeit 15 years old, of proposed legislation drafted for U.S. Congressional approval.

NOTES ON REPARATIONS FOR NEW AFRIKANS IN AMERICA

Prepared for September 11, 1987 Workshop of the National Conference of Black Lawyers

By **Chokwe Lumumba**
Chairman of the New Afrikan People's Organization
Attorney at Law

Copyright Chokwe Lumumba 1987.

INTRODUCTION

What follows is a brief survey of the factual basis, legal analysis, and historical precedents for the present demand for the payment by the United States of reparations to descendants of Afrikans held as slaves (New Afrikans) in America. This short paper is being submitted along with a written contribution on the subject by the Minister of Justice of the Provisional Government of the Republic of New Afrika, Attorney Nkechi Taifa, entitled "Reparations and Self-Determination." Also included with this submission is a proposed reparation bill prepared by Dr. Imari Obadele, I, the President of the Provisional Government of the Republic of New Afrika. It is submitted on behalf of Dr. Obadele and myself. Finally I am submitting to the workshop at the request of the planners of the conference a proposed Reparation Amendment to the United States Constitution.

President Obadele, Attorney Taifa, and I believe that reparations payments to New Afrikans require no Constitutional Amendment. The Thirteenth Amendment of the Constitution of the United States is a constitutional basis for the reparation bill. The Thirteenth Amendment provides as follows:

Section 1. Neither slavery nor involuntary servitude except as a punishment for crime whereof the party shall have been duly convicted, shall exist within the United States, or any place subject to their jurisdiction.

Section 2. Congress shall have power to enforce this article by appropriate legislation. U.S. Const. Amend. 13.

Section one of this amendment abolished all shades and conditions of Afrikan slavery. Slaughter-House Cases, 16 Wall. 36, 17 (1873).

Section two gives Congress the right to eliminate all shades, conditions, badges, and incidents of slavery by all appropriate legislation. United States v. Harris, 106 U.S. 629 (1883).

The loss of the benefit of two hundred years of forced labor and deprivation of liberty and life, not to mention the theft of black genius during and after slavery, and invidious discrimination after slavery, are incidents of slavery. These incidents and other badges of slavery have deprived the New Afrikan population of considerable wealth, and left the black masses in wretched social and economic conditions. In fact slavery and its progeny have left the vast majority of New Afrikans in worse condition than the white population. Consequently, reparations could be legislated by the Congress under the 13tth Amendment in order to alleviate the vestiges of slavery.

HISTORY OF THE NEW AFRIKAN (BLACK) REPARATION DEMAND

New Afrikans in America have consistently demanded reparations from the United States Government or other American institutions. In addition to those demands noted by Sister Nkechi Taifa in her paper, the following should be noted.

1. The historical demand for 40 acres for ex-slaves was expressed in the United States House of Representatives and the Senate by Thaddeus Stevens and Charles Sumner, respectively. These radical Republicans did not create the demand for land by Afrikans in America. Historian Lerone Bennett Jr. points out that the mass demand for land by freemen after and during the Civil War was manifest. W.E.B. Du Bois describes the post-Civil War land rebellions fought by freemen in their struggle for land and survival in the southeast of the country. In fact New Afrikans fought U.S. Marshalls in an effort to retain control of independent New Afrikan communities shortly after the Civil War.

2. Longtime New Afrikan political activist and reparation researcher Christopher Alston in Detroit has accumulated an historic exhibit comprised of old news articles, letters, and various other documents which detail the history of a late 1800s, early 1900s black reparation organization which organized tens of thousands of New Afrikans behind the demand for reparation.

3. In addition to the demand by the Provisional Government of the Republic of New Afrika in the

late 60s as indicated by Attorney Taifa, reparations were demanded by the National Black Economic Development Conference in 1969.

4. In 1972, 10,000 Black delegates gathered at the Black National Convention in Gary, Indiana, and adopted a Black Agenda which specifically called for reparations to Blacks in America from the U.S. government. The Black Agenda also recognized the right of the Republic of New Afrika to political independence and sovereignty over Black Belt land in the southeast.

5. Currently Sister Dorothy Lewis, former Chairperson of the National Black Reparations Organization; the Provisional Government of the Republic of New Afrika; the New Afrikan People's Organization; the Afrikan National Reparations Organization, and numerous other political formations and individuals are organizing people around a call for reparations.

FACTS AND LAW SUPPORT THE REPARATIONS DEMAND

The horrible history of the slave trade, slavery and countless other human rights violations perpetrated upon the New Afrikan population are the subject of many books. Moreover, reference to any reasonably accurate indicator of the economic, social, educational, and political status and condition of New Afrikans in America today demonstrates both the contemporary impact of these historic horrors and the current existence of colonial oppression of New Afrikans by political and economic U.S. powers. In fact the New Afrikan condition is steadily deteriorating under U.S. control. Attorney Daisy G. Collins has authored an excellent review of the facts and the law pertinent to reparations for

Afrikans in America. This work appears in a *Howard Law Journal* in 1970.

Sister Collins cites historical facts in the modern statistics which demonstrate the badges of slavery attached to the New African population. Collins explains that reparation is the "redress for an injury, amends for wrong inflicted." She asserts that the discrimination against New Africans is actually so well-established as to be a fact worthy of judicial notice. She also notes that the fact that wrongs have continued a long-time does not justify them, nor does it mitigate the liability. "There is no such thing as a vested right to do wrong." Johannesen v. United States, 225 U.S. 227 (1912).

Sister Collins also notes that Article I and 55 of the United States Charter both refer to the principles of equal rights, self-determination of peoples, and to human rights and fundamental freedoms without distinction as to race. Collins states that as a signatory to the Charter, the United States is obligated to remove all racial inequality for which it is responsible.

Sister Collins also notes that the Universal Declaration of Human Rights imposes obligations on the United States to eliminate all forms and relics of slavery and to afford all in its jurisdiction an adequate standard of living. Collins notes that the U.S. failure to meet these obligations supports the Black reparation claim.

Sister Collins also makes various U.S. Constitutional arguments for reparations. She argues that thru slavery and invidious discrimination, New Africans have been deprived of property without due process of law in violation of the 5th and 14th Amendments. One might add, the New Afrikans have likewise been deprived of life and liberty without due process. Sister Collins reaches the 13th Amendment question, and like the present author, argues that the 13th is the proper constitutional basis for reparation legislation.

Collins furthermore argues that the 14th Amendment provides a basis for reparation. She notes that section 1 of that Amendment supposedly "makes" blacks citizens of the United States, while Section 5 gives Congress power to enforce by appropriate legislation, the provisions of this article. Collins thus argues that reparations are necessary to secure economic rights for blacks sufficient for parity with the whites. By so doing the 14th Amendment "makes" New Afrikans (Blacks) citizens of the United States.

REPARATION AND SELF-DETERMINATION

The latter point in Sister Collins' excellent work is troublesome. She seems to assume that "making" New Afrikan citizens of the United States is both desirable and consistent with reparation and human rights principles previously discussed. Both assumptions are wrong.

"Making" a free people citizens without their informed consent is a limitation on that people's freedom. If the informed consent exists from the population in question, then the population is "made" citizens, but have become citizens under their own volition.

The imposition of US citizenship on New Afrikans without their express consent offends our human right to self-determination, and leaves true realization of other human rights in doubt and/or in jeopardy. The distinction between making us citizens of the U.S. and voluntary *choice* of such citizenship, by New Afrikans desiring the same, is important. First, many of us do not want to be citizens of the United States. In fact history suggests that this has been the case since the inception of the United States (i.e. Denmark Vesey, Gabriel Prosser, Nat Turner, Henry Garnett, Afrikan blood Brotherhood, Marcus Garvey, Nation of Islam, etc.).

Second, it should be noted that an imposition on those of us (New Afrikans) not desiring the same is a badge of slavery. But for our enslavement no such "citizenship" could be imposed.

Third, imposed citizenship offends the 13th Amendment. It limits the freedom declared by that amendment, and subjects many so called free persons to an unwanted political status, merely by virtue of their presence in the United States – a presence which emanates from the enslavement that the 13th Amendment is purported to have abolished. No person or population so disposed can be said to have received full reparation for slavery.

The political essence of slavery is not merely found in economic exploitation of labor, but in the illegal and imposition of United States jurisdiction on the slave, or the slave's descendants. Full reparation must relieve those imposed upon of *any* political status *forced* on them. Recall that Sister Collins has appropriately defined reparation as "redress for an injury, or amends for a wrong inflicted." A wrong doer certainly cannot amend for a wrong inflicted, by inflicting another wrong.

In order to interpret the 14th Amendment in a manner consistent with the international right to self-determination, and consistent with the 13th Amendment, the 14th Amendment's declaration on citizenship must be viewed as an offer of citizenship which Congress through appropriate legislation must extend to New Afrikans. Properly interpreted the Amendment does not require imposition of U.S. citizenship on New Afrikans.

PROPOSED REPARATION AMENDMENT

1. All descendants of Afrikans (New Afrikans, Liberians, etc.) previously held in slavery within the United States and its occupied territories during any period of time when the laws of the United States, or any states thereof, protected and/or permitted this enslavement and all descendants of Africans transported in slave commerce permitted under United States law, or the law of any state which is part of the United States shall be entitled collectively and individually, to reparations from the United States government and full compensation for all physical, educational, economic, political, cultural, and mental loss and injuries that such Afrikan descendants have suffered as a consequence of their Afrikan ancestors' enslavement. All such persons shall also be collectively and individually entitled to reparations from the United States government and full compensation for injury and loss due to all other violations of their human rights, or the human rights of their ancestors, by the United States government, by any state of the United States, or by individuals subject to United States or state laws, whose commission of such violations were allowed by, and known to, or which should have been known to officials of the United

States government, or to government officials of a state of the United States.

2. This Amendment shall require payment of reparations by the United States Government directly to individual Afrikan descendants entitled under this Amendment, to representatives of Organizations chosen by the entitled persons and to the Afrikan states and Nations in the Western Hemisphere and Afrika to which the entitled persons belong. In addition to reparations payments received on behalf of entitled individuals, and groups, the Republic of New Afrika and any Afrikan state shall be entitled to reparations for any damages suffered as a nation or state, because of slavery, the slave trade and other human rights violations perpetrated by the United States or one of its states against the nationals of these nations or states, or against their ancestors. This Amendment shall allow such nations or states reparation for belligerent acts committed against them by the United States, or any state organization, or individual operating under United States authority or protection, where the Act was designed to facilitate the continuation of slavery, the slave trade or other human rights violations against Afrikans, or their descendants.

3. Reparations under this Amendment shall be paid and money with interest, and machinery, technology, land and in any other appropriate form as determined by the United States Congress, after consultation with representatives of the Afrikan Nations, states, and individuals entitled to reparations payments. The amount to be paid shall also be determined by Congress after such consultation.

4. The United States and each state of the United States and each individual under its jurisdiction shall hereafter recognize and respect the human rights of all persons and nations, including those entitled to reparations under this Amendment. Such recognition and respect shall include an absolute recognition of the right of Afrikan descendants (New Afrikans) in the United States and its occupied territories, to self-determination. Thus neither the government of the United States or the various states, nor individuals under the jurisdiction shall restrict the right of New Afrikans to (a) repatriate to Afrika, (b) emigrate to another country, (c) become full citizens of the United States, or (d) establish an independent nation state in the New Afrikan territory in America.

5. The United States, the states of the United States, and individuals under United States jurisdiction shall make no effort to impose United States citizenship on Afrikan descendants in America and elsewhere.

6. To the extent that any prior provision of this constitution is inconsistent with this amendment it is hereby repealed.

7. Congress shall have the power to enact the appropriate legislation and take necessary steps to implement and enforce the provisions of this amendment.

REPARATIONS YES!

A Suggestion Towards the Framework of A Reparations Demand And A Set of Legal Underpinnings

By Imari Abubakari Obadele
Chairperson, the People's Center Council (National Legislature)
of the Provisional Government
Republic of New Afrika
And Associate Professor of Political Science,
Prairie View A&M University, Texas

I. GENERAL OUTLINE OF THE CASE FOR REPARATIONS

THIS paper is a suggestion toward the elaboration of a viable framework for the campaign for reparations, which are to be paid to the descendants of persons held as slaves in North America, by the United States government. It offers a set of legal/political underpinnings which may prove useful as a point of departure and making a compelling, logical case.

Annexed to this paper is a lean, proposed draft of legislation, which could be used as an initial framework for a bill in Congress. Like the proffered legal/political case which follows, the draft reparations legislation is a beginning, not the conclusion.

Where one distinguished author on the case for reparations, Professor Boris I. Bittker, would have us forsake claims for reparations based on slavery and focus on claims arising since *Plessy V. Ferguson*, this paper argues that reparations are due us from both slavery and post-slavery activities of the United States Government. The focus of this paper, however, is on claims arising from our enslavement.

This is not to say that post-slavery claims are unimportant. They are quite important and a necessary part of our total package. In fact, during the past two decades a form of reparations has been won by a scattering of legal claimants and union activists attacking post-slavery discrimination in the United States' economic structure, although neither claimants nor repairs have used the term *reparation*. Recall that the *Weber* case arose in the context of an affirmative action plan between the United Steelworkers of America and the Kaiser Aluminum Company, which sought to have the number of New Afrikans (i.e. "Black people") in the skilled trades at each plant reach a number equivalent to the number of New Afrikans in the local work force. To achieve this, 50% of the places in pre-apprentice training classes were reserved for New Afrikans. In the words of Justice Brennan, who wrote the opinion finding the plan lawful, the plan was designed "to eliminate conspicuous racial imbalances in Kaiser's then almost exclusively white craft work forces."

In the first week of September (1987) the state of Ohio deferred settlement of one-half of an NAACP lawsuit which asked back-pay and other provisions for New Afrikans who had been discriminated against and employment opportunities with that state›s prisons. Ohio did, however, settle the half of the suit which applied to women generally, agreeing to a payment of $3.75 million for women who had been denied jobs, or assignments at certain prisons. The settlement figure is largely for back-pay and (for women not hired) missed pay. This settlement gives promise of a later settlement based purely upon racial discrimination.

On May 12, 1987, Judge Barrington Parker of the U.S. District Court, Washington D.C., approved a back-pay settlement in a ten-year-old racial discrimination, class-action suit, which totaled $2.4 million dollars. It covered 350 present and former New Afrikan employees of the U.S. Government Printing Office. Essentially the back-pay award was to compensate for salaries which would have been earned had there been no racial discrimination in promotions and assignment to journeyman positions. Earlier, in 1981, the judge had imposed goals and timetables for promotions. These were met.

A similar settlement was won by Attorney Raymond Willis and other lawyers more than a decade ago against Bell Telephone of Michigan. There have been others since then.

Such settlements by private companies, as opposed to the United States or state governments, bear a resemblance to the private company settlements which have appeared in the scheme of West German reparations for victims of the Nazi regime. A year ago, for instance, Feldmuehlel Nobel announced it would pay the equivalent of $2 million to Jews who worked as slave laborers in the industrial concern under the Nazi regime.

I wish only to emphasize that post-slavery reparations claims, even if arguably stopped with events occurring in 1968, when the American state structure no longer contained racially discriminatory laws, are an important area for our proper attention. (See the "present value" work of Professor Richard F. America and other economists, who calculate reparations owed for the effects of slavery, poor health, lack of education, and other factors depriving New Afrikans of our earnings.)

I turn here to the question of slavery-based reparations claims because of the enormity – duration and inhumanity – of the acts committed against us during the era of slavery and the failure of the United States government, which gave the sanction and protection of the law to those acts and their perpetrators, to make any sincere and comprehensive attempt at rehabilitation and compensation, and consultation with us.

We who make the claim of reparations due for slavery are mindful of the disdain heaped upon our charges by people like Professor Bittker. "The preoccupation with slavery," Bittker writes, "has stultified the discussion of black reparations by implying that the only issue is the correction of an ancient Injustice, thus inviting the reply that the wrongs were committed by persons long since dead, whose profits may well have dissipated during their own lifetimes or their descendants' and whose moral responsibility should not be visited on succeeding generations, let alone wholly unrelated persons." Bittker goes on to quote Robert Penn Warren asking whether "an Athenian helot of the fifth century B.C.... [would] have a claim today on the Greek government." Warren adds: "how many explosion-prone trade guns, ankers of rum and iron bars the Nigerian government owes what percentage of the twenty million American Negroes" for their role in capturing and then selling us? "The whole thing is a grisly farce. Come to think of it, it smacks not of fantasy but of bedlam."

Such poorly disguised hostility towards righting a monstrous wrong against our people well suggests why in the past none of our serious efforts for reparations, even when aided by well intentioned Whites, has so far succeeded. This is so whether We hark back to the question of forty acres and a mule inserted by our friends in Congress into a Freedmen's Bureau bill and vetoed by Andrew Jackson (and not overridden by the Congress) or to our many efforts since then. This opposition by "liberal" Whites remains a practical obstacle of large magnitude.

While insisting that We should seek no redress for events which occurred only 120 years ago, none of these gentlemen, including Mr. Bittker, has seen fit to suggest that the inheritance laws in the United States be changed so that everyone who is benefiting from a legacy accumulated 120 years ago forgoes it. I found no indication in Mr. Bittker's book that he or his associates, any of whom were benefiting from 120-year-old legacies, had volunteered to give them up. I see no need to argue the fact that labor was stolen from our people (although there are scholars arguing the amount and relating that to conditions of poor White workers), but i will make further comments sustaining the suggestion that reparations are due not just for stolen labor but for unjust war and cultural aggression. Whatever the amount owed, that amount constitutes a legacy, never paid, and due to the heirs.

To help put the 120 years into perspective, it is useful to know that Justice Thurgood Marshall is said to be the great grandson of a person held as a slave. While Justice Marshall is a few years older than i, i nevertheless remember my grandfather well, and he was born just as slavery ended, assuring that some of his relatives, perhaps even older siblings, had been held as slaves. It is relevant, moreover, that the heritage which Mr. Bittker and other Whites enjoy in this country, even the immigrants, is what has been called white skin privilege: they benefit from a society, state, and economic structure which are governed by White supremacy – except for the state structure which ceased to be so governed only a decade ago – and while all of us may debate ingenious methods of operationalizing this data for measurement, there is no question that Whites in this country enjoy the fruits of 300 years of White supremacy. As a nation the Whites have been unjustly enriched by our stolen labor and succored by our degradation. White individuals have partaken of all of this.

The central proposition of this paper and the draft bill for reparations which is annexed hereto is that our enslavement in the 13 colonies and the United States was a matter of war – war conducted against Afrika under authority, initially, of the British government and the legislators of the Thirteen Colonies and ultimately under authority of Clause One, Section 9 of the First Article of the United States Constitution. It was war conducted against Afrikan people – who grew into a nation, an oppressed nation, between 1660 and 1860 - within the United States under British and Colonial authority and, ultimately the authority of Clause Three, Section Two of Article Four of the U.S. Constitution.

The conditions of our degradation, a subordinated and exploited people denied liberty by force, are too well known to be re-documented or chronicled here. Justice Harlan, writing his dissent in the *Civil Rights Cases*, 109 U.S. 3, at 29, said that the provisions of the 1850 "Fugitive Slave Act … placed at the disposal of the master seeking to recover his fugitive slave, substantially the whole power of the nation." The U.S. Army under Andrew Jackson destroyed the New Afrikan States in Florida. Militia and White civilians carried war to all our communities in the woods. The U.S. military and White civilians put down the attempts of, first, Gabriel Prosser and then Denmark Vesey and John Brown and Osborne Anderson to seize land and build New Afrikan states. For these state-builders the U.S. courts authorized bloody executions, corporal punishment, and transportation beyond U.S. shores. Moreover, the courts and executive functionaries coldly carried out the inhumane re-enslavement of inoffensive persons who had simply slipped away quietly from slavery doing harm to no one, seeking only a degree more freedom in the North.

It is the proposition of this paper, embracing propositions enunciated by the Provisional Government of the Republic of New Afrika sixteen years ago, that the United States conducted war against the New Afrikan nation on this land throughout the era of slavery, that the war was authorized by the United States constitution and carried out in aggressive military actions against the efforts of our people to speak freedom individually and to build New Afrikan states collectively, by the United States government Itself, by the various State Governments and by civilians mobilized against the New Afrikan people and Nation.

It is the proposition of this paper that reparations must be part of a general settlement of the war which the United States has waged against us. In keeping with settlements consummated at the end of World War I and World War II, and with the precedents in International Law created by these settlements, the settlement for New Afrikan people must include not simply money reparations but exercise of the free and informed right to self-determination by our people, and the release of our militants, *soldiers, prisoners of war*, now in U.S. jails, who were taken in defense of our nation against the United States.

 In summary, the money damages are due, of course, for labor stolen from our forebears, for cultural assault, and for unjust war, with accumulated interest. But the money portion of our reparations must be a significant contribution towards *rehabilitation: repatriation* for those who wish and can achieve citizenship in an Afrikan state, *rehabilitation* of the New Afrikan states and incipient states, and their successors, destroyed on this soil during the war which was slavery, and afterwards. There must be reparation payments for rehabilitation of us as a people, our social structure in the United States, and culture, in recognition of the design followed in the United States to make us into a race of ignorant subservients, unable to revolt, and forgetful that We had a duty to do so. Lerone Bennett, writing in his *Confrontation: Black and White* (Baltimore: Penguin Books, 1966, pages 26-27), gives one compelling summary of some aspects of the cultural aggressions for which reparations are due. He writes:

> Anticipating the devious tactics of the modern police state, master's laid hands on the minds of their chattel. By the old method of the carrot and the stick, by terror and by smiles, by whips, chains, words, symbols, prayers, and curses, the Negro was taught to "stand in fear" of white power.

> In some such manner, Afrikans were given a new conception of themselves, a conception that carried as core – elements guilt, anxiety, and inferiority. The laying of hands on the mind of a whole people,

the pulling out by the roots of old customs and habits, continued for hundreds of years. Hundreds of thousands died in the process, and hundreds of thousands went insane. But millions survived, maimed to be sure, shrunken, shriven, diminue but, withal, alive and breathing...

There are reparations due to certain Afrikan states for the war which the United States authorized against them; to us, as well, for our states that were weakened or destroyed in Afrika during the course of America's war there, which resulted in our enslavement. (A state, with its Army, protects the people. People cannot be harmed by outsiders unless the army is destroyed, rendered ineffective, or co-opted.) And it is also true that discussions must be held with Nigeria and other states on reparations for us. These could involve not simply trade arrangements but substantial political and diplomatic assistance for those of us who want independent statehood.

Those discussions are separate, however, from the claims against the United States and the subject of this paper.

The precedents for the claims described above are to be found in:

1. The agreements which concluded World War I and World War II;

2. The U.S. Supreme Court case, The United States v. The Libellants and Claimants of the Schooner Amistad, 15 Peters 518 (1841);

3. the New International Law Regime, which took its rise with the Declaration on the Granting of

Independence to Colonial Countries and Peoples, United Nations General Assembly Resolution 1514, 14 December 1960, and

4. the principles involved in the work of The Indian Claims Commission, Title 25, U.S.C.A., Sections 70 et seq.

With respect to the lapse of time between the United States' initial ceasefire against us (The Thirteenth Amendment of December 1865) and Queen Mother Moore›s proffer of the Ethiopian Woman›s complaint against the United States and petition for reparations to the United Nations in 1963, three comments are particularly appropriate. First, Queen Mother Moore›s efforts were not a beginning; at no substantial period during the era since slavery have our people neglected wholly the campaign for reparations. Second, it has been the power of the United States and its refusal to consider reparations for New Afrikans which has frustrated our efforts heretofore, not any failure on our part to pursue these demands.

This is relevant to the legal doctrine of laches. Based upon the maxim that equity aids the vigilant and not those who slumber on their rights, the doctrine of laches operates against one who neglects to assert a claim when such neglect, considered with the passage of time, harms the adverse party. Laches could, of course, become applicable where it is the heir of the party against whom the claim is asserted, rather than the actual offending party. Justice Paul Stevens of the U.S. Supreme Court, writing the dissent in *County of Oneida, New York v. Oneida Nation*, 470 U.S. 226, 264 (4 March 1985), arguing that a claim of the 1795 transaction should have been barred by laches, put it this way: "the Court recognized that the long passage of time, the change in the character of the property, the transfer of some of the property to third parties, the absence of any obvious inadequacy in the consideration received in the original transaction, and Patrick's lack of direct participation in the original transfer all supported a charge of laches against the plaintiffs." (Of course, hardly anyone would argue that there was any *adequacy* in the consideration – i.e., pay and room and board – provided persons held in America as slaves.)

In this case the Supreme Court majority was unconvinced that laches could be applied and pointedly emphasized that Congress should act in such matters. The Court added: "One would have thought that claims dating back more than a century and a half would have been barred long ago. As our opinion indicates, however, neither petitioners nor we have found any applicable statute of limitations or other relevant legal basis for holding that the Oneidas' claims are barred or otherwise have been satisfied." *County of Oneida v. Oneida Nation*, at 253.

Finally, and as a matter of international practice, it should be noted that under the Franco-German peace treaty of 10 May 1871, the French lost an area known as Alsace-Lorraine, and many French citizens, resident in Alsace-Lorraine, lost French citizenship. Fifty years later, under the Versailles Treaty which ended World War I and went into force on 10 January 1920, France not only received Alsace-Lorraine once more but reinstated French Citizenship. Only the Germans batted an eye.

II. WAS IT WAR AND DO WE HAVE SELF-DETERMINATION RIGHTS?

Two essential questions should be addressed. First, was it war? Second, do New Afrikans have self-determination rights? Also implicated is the question as to whether New Afrikans in the United States constitute a "nation." We now turn to the first question.

In general, "war" has been held to be generally of two types, conflicts between states, which are governed by international law and practice, and civil wars, in which part of a state contends for sovereignty over territory claimed by the parent-state. Lately conflicts of liberation movements, including conflicts like that in South Afrika at the present time, where the liberation forces are unable to place armies openly in the field or to hold and govern territory openly, have gained status under the international law. The 1977 Protocol to the Geneva Conventions of 1949, states in Article One:

> 4. The situations referred to in the preceding paragraph include armed conflicts in which peoples are fighting against colonial domination and alien occupation and against racist regimes in the exercise of their right to self-determination, as enshrined in the Charter of the United Nations and the Declaration on Principles of International Law concerning Friendly Relations and Co-operation among states in accordance with the Charter of the United Nations.

The record is replete with instances of armed conflict and armed suppression of suspected militants by the United States, during and after slavery. Moreover, the general conditions of slavery make clear also that We were subject during the slavery era to "colonial domination and alien occupation." When one considers the persistent action of the United States and its political subdivisions against our communities in the woods and against the Apalachicola and Seminole states in Florida, against Tunis Campbell's state, set up on Sapelo and St. Catherine's islands, off Georgia after the Civil War, the words of Justice Johnson, concurring in decision against the Cherokee in Cherokee Nation v. State of Georgia, 5 Peters 1, 28-29, come readily to mind:

> That in pursuance of those laws the functionaries of Georgia have entered their territory with an armed force and put down all powers, legislative, executive, and judicial, exercised under the government of the Indians.

> What does this series of allegations exhibit but a state of war, and the fact of invasion? They allege themselves to be a sovereign independent State, and set out that another sovereign State has by its laws, its functionaries, and its armed force, invaded their State and put down their authority. This is war in fact; though not being declared with the usual solemnities, it may be perhaps be [sic] called war in disguise.

Professor von Glahn notes that "a British report in 1870 showed that between 1700 and 1870, a total of 107 conflicts had been initiated without the formality of a declaration of war." He goes on: "The United States, too, has conducted wars without a declaration: an undeclared war with France from 1798 to 1801, the invasion of Florida in 1811 under

Generals Jackson and Mathews, the brief Mexican invasion in 1916, the undeclared war with the Soviet Union in 1918-1919, and, of course, the Vietnamese conflict from 1947 onward (for the United States, from March 7, 1965, to March 29, 1973). [Footnote omitted."]

The effort of some New Afrikans to form an independent state has been an almost continuous effort from the time of our first flights and revolts in this land to the present. The state-building of Tunis Campbell had hardly been put down when Henry Adams and his associates in Louisiana and Mississippi began their appeals to Congress for "land anywhere." Edward McCabe's efforts to make Oklahoma a black state (initially at least, within the U.S. federal union), preceded the work of Marcus Garvey by more than a generation, but there is a linkage between Marcus Garvey and Elijah Muhammad and Al Hajj Al Malik Shabazz, Malcolm X. Malcolm's work gave birth to the Provisional Government, Republic of New Afrika, which today and since 1968 has led the effort for the establishment of an independent New Afrikan state in Mississippi and four other Deep South states.

If the level of U.S. military attacks against New Afrikans and the New Afrikan nation receded in the period following the Civil War, our colony was nevertheless subject to a racially conscious policing by sheriffs and local police. The army, too, would appear to suppress us during uprisings such as those in 1919, the 1940s, and the 1960s. The reason for the reduction in naked military attacks lay mainly in our resort to parliamentary means of struggle, after the Civil War. But there was no abandonment of the drive for independent New Afrikan statehood - nor for the other two objectives toward which some of our people had striven traditionally: (1) full citizenship in the United States, and (2) return to Afrika.

It is relevant to the charge of war against the United States that We were still an occupied and oppressed nation in this period between the Civil War and 1968. We were a colony living on territory claimed by the United States, subject until 1968 to a body of legislation and court decisions which defined our subordination to the White nation and facilitated the White nation's economic and cultural exploitation of us, and our social degradation.

Even the Malcolmites, who after March 1968 led the struggle for independent statehood and were resolute practitioners of armed self-defense, eventually supported by the Black Liberation Army, pursued a strategy of attempting to organize, peacefully, an independence plebiscite. This parliamentary strategy was in accordance with the precepts of the New International Law Regime, ushered in by the United Nations' *Declaration On the Granting of Independence to Colonial Countries and Peoples, supra,* in 1960. When the organizing of the armed, self-defending cadres of the Provisional Government accelerated in Mississippi in 1971, however, the United States turned to its military option. At dawn on Wednesday, August 18, 1971, a force of FBI agents and Jackson city police, accompanied by an armored truck, attacked the official RNA Provisional Government Residence. They shot it up and then charged the seven occupants of the house, along with the four who had spent the night at the office several blocks away, with murder of the police lieutenant who died in the attack and with assault of the FBI agent and the policeman who were wounded. In the fall of 1981 the United States brought massive military force to bear in McComb County, Mississippi, to arrest Sister Fulani

Sunni Ali, a longtime RNA officer, who was quietly conducting a summer camp for children in the country. The pretext was the New York Brinks incident, during which Black Liberation Army members, were implicated, some arrested and some jailed, and one murdered in cold blood by the police as he lay helpless on the ground.

If it is possible to argue that the *form* of the war against us changed, after the Civil War, from military activity to occupation duties, the United States military sanction was always ready - and, from time to time, used it.

The question was *land*. The United States Government, unable to export us *en masse* after the Civil War, was not especially concerned that U.S. policies had fueled our growth as a separate people - giving us our own perspective and history and common gene pool, raising up, between 1660 and 1860, a vastly outnumbered New Afrikan nation on this soil. Our status as a nation despite our numbers posed little more problem for the United States than the many Indian nations - so long as We did not focus overly on our separateness and nationhood, and so long as We did not seriously act for *statehood*, for sovereignty over land.

The international law, in our era before 1960, was shaped by Europeans and their conquests. This included the question of sovereignty over land, national title to land. And the law was clear. For instance, the principle of prescription still means that a state may acquire title over land originally belonging to another state, by occupation over a long period of time. How long is a long time? There seems to be no generally accepted international standard. One U.S. court decision, dealing with awards to Indian states, determined that title to land could be recognized for a group which had occupied it uninterruptedly for 50 years. The United States objective with respect to the RNA Provisional Government (PG-RNA) was to prevent undisturbed occupation for *any* period of time.

There is little doubt that the United States realized that a form of the prescription principle is embedded in the New Afrikan Creed, which today is part of the Republic's constitution, the Code of Umoja, and which is recited by gathered Provisional Government cadre at meetings and all important occasions. "I believe," runs the paragraph from the Creed, "that all the land in America, upon which We have lived for a long time, which We have worked and built upon, and which We have fought to stay on, is land that belongs to us as a people." That claim is constitutionally subject to the just claims of the Indians. There is little doubt that the United States understood that the PG was acting upon this principle in Mississippi.

The particular problem for the United States was that the Provisional Government had been created at a founding convention and then regularly elected, by popular vote since 1975. Although the voting has always taken place in several cities, the totals, so far, have always been small - the largest being 5,000 votes cast in 1975. But the fact of the vote and the potential for it becoming a widespread institution among New Afrikan people, despite the perpetual press "white-out" of New Afrikan activities, posed and pose a serious problem for United States policy-makers. To begin with, the United States is a party to the 1933 Convention on the Rights and Duties of States, done at Montevideo, Uruguay. This convention's definition of the "state" is in fact the definition which has entered into the principles of United

States law, repeated in numerous contexts. Article one of the convention states:

> The state as a person of international law should possess the following qualifications: (a) a permanent population; (b) a defined territory; (c) government; and (d) the capacity to enter into relations with the other states.

The Provisional Government was (and is) a democratically elected government; it was voted for in Mississippi, which testified to representation of a permanent population, and it carried on various nascent forms of relations with China and Cuba (and, in the days since the Mississippi effort of the 1970s, is continuing to broaden these relations with other states). What was lacking, then, to convert this state-building entity, the Provisional Government, into a state was uninterrupted possession of *land*.

The United States' attack on the Provisional Government in Mississippi and the subsequent major de-stabilization of the Provisional Government by the jailing of some of its leaders and a continuation of the FBI's disinformation campaign (the *COINTELPRO*) were simply consistent with the attacks in former days on Gabriel Prosser, Denmark Vesey, John Brown and Osborne Perry Anderson, the New Afrikan states in Florida, and the state of Tunis Campbell. The rationale was simple and obvious: the United States, which into this century was completing the process of driving Indians from seats of sovereignty from sea to shining sea, from the Canadian border to Mexico and the Gulf, was not prepared to abide the creation of an independent New Afrikan state in North America. Thus, the attacks, the recurrent hot war.

But there was a difference in the international law regime under which the military actions against the New Afrikan states and state-builders *before* 1960 were carried out and the international law regime under which U.S. military attacks against the Provisional Government were carried out *after* 1960. The *Decolonization Declaration* (U.N. Gen. Assembly Res. 1514) said, simply, that "All peoples have the right to self-determination; by virtue of that right they freely determine their political status and freely pursue their economic, social and cultural development." This language has been carried over into the human rights conventions. It was a victory of the Afro-Asian bloc in the General Assembly, achieving numerical prominence for the first time in 1960, and it marked a revolution in international law. The Declaration states also: "4. *All armed action or repressive measures of all kinds directed against dependent peoples shall cease in order to enable them to exercise peacefully and freely their right to complete independence...*" The Declaration makes liberation struggles lawful and, possibly, peaceful.

Therefore the international law that counted had been written and accepted by the United States and European powers. It served the ratification of their conquests of the rest of the world and codified practices which *they* had found to be mutually convenient. The Versailles Treaty of 1920, ending World War I, joins the Berlin Treaty of 1885, as a leading statement of the international law as the White and powerful states of the world saw it and enforced it. This document provided for our degradation: it left the Afrikan and Asian *colonies* of the World War I victors in place and, instead of freeing those held by the defeated Germany, *gave* our hapless countries and peoples to the mandated "care" of Britain, France and Belgium - at the same time that this treaty was concretizing *self-determination* as a right for Czechs and Poles and several other peoples in Europe.

The Afro-Asians in 1960, with the assistance of Canada and a few other states, re-wrote the international law. From that point, not only Europeans but *all* peoples had a right to self-determination. A subsequent, relatively rapid development of the law followed. The principle of self-determination was incorporated in United Nations General Assembly Resolution 2625, *The Declaration on Principles of International Law*, on 24 October 1970.

The United States abstained from voting on the 1960 Declaration, objecting to the word "independence" in the title, arguing that independence was not the only possible result of an act of self-determination by a people. This was true but irrelevant. Nevertheless, the United States Representative, James J. Wadsworth, speaking to a plenary session of the U.N. General Assembly on 6 December 1960 made the following extraordinary remarks - which of course, under U.S. constitutional principles, are deemed to be the words of the U.S. president and an authoritative statement of international law as the United States views it:

> First let me say what we mean by colonialism ...It is the imposition of alien power over a people, usually by force and without the free and formal consent of the governed. It is the perpetuation of that power. It is the denial of the right of self-determination - whether by suppressing free-expression or by withholding necessary educational, economic, and social development. *** Obviously not all colonial regimes have been the same .... but, however important these differences are, the fact remains that colonialism in

any form is undesirable. Neither the most benevolent paternalism by a ruling power nor the most grateful acceptance of these benefits by indigenous leaders can meet the test of the charter or satisfy the spirit of this age.

The Declaration on the Principles of International Law in its "principle of equal rights and self determination of peoples," states, inter-alia:

Every State has the duty to promote, through joint and separate action, the realization of the principle of equal rights and self determination ... bearing in mind that subjugation of peoples to alien subjugation, domination and exploitation constitutes a violation of the principle, as well as a denial of fundamental human rights, and is contrary to the Charter of the United Nations.

The establishment of a sovereign and independent State, the free association or integration with an independent State or the emergence into any other political status freely determined by a people constitute modes of implementing the right of self-determination by that people.

Now the United States' ratification of concepts contained in the two cited declarations does not rest, alone, upon Ambassador Wadsworth's extraordinary 1960 remarks. Mr. Reagan's administration, in arguing in favor of the commonwealth and free association arrangements which the United States was implementing with the Marshall and Mariana Islands - part of the "Strategic Trust" of the Pacific mandated to the United States after World War II - explicitly embraced the self-determination formulation contained in the Declaration on the Principles of International Law.

THERE is, of course, the important question here as to whether or not New Afrikans constitute a "people" and a *nation* within the contemplation of the self-determination provisions of the international law and/or standards of domestic law binding, arguably, on the United States.

Our right to international law rights, i argue, was in fact established by the United States Supreme Court nearly 150 years before Ambassador Feldman embraced the self-determination principle in the *Declaration on the Principles of International Law*. This was done by the court's ruling in the *Amistad* case, *supra*.

In 1825, 36 years after the present U.S. Constitution had gone into effect and 18 years after that Constitution had banned the slave trade, Chief Justice John Marshall, while expressing abhorrence at the trade, refused to acknowledge, for Afrikans brought before him after being taken in the illegal trade, any right to self-determination. Justice Marshall reasoned that while Great Britain and the United States had abandoned the horrid trade and were inveighing upon other states to do so, all other countries had *not* yet done so. Thus, he wrote: "the legality of the capture of a vessel engaged in the slave-trade depends on the law of the country to which the vessel belongs. If that law gives its sanction to the trade, restitution will be decreed; if that law prohibits it, the vessel and cargo will be condemned as a good prize." *The Antelope*, 23 U.S. (10 Wheat.) 66.

But 16 years later the United States Supreme Court, faced again with a group of Afrikans who had reached these shores after having been taken in the illegal slave trade, was able to find in them the right individually to self-determination. In the *Amistad* case the Afrikans had successfully revolted on shipboard and were in command of the vessel when they and it were seized by a small U.S. naval force off Long Island, New York. U.S. Navy Lieutenant Gedney had sued for salvage. Spain and the private owners had asked return of the ship and the Afrikans, as slaves. The United States asked that the Afrikans be turned over to the U.S. President for return to the coast of Afrika in accordance with the act of March 3, 1819, mandating such treatment for persons freed by the United States in the illegal slave trade.

Justice Story, delivering the opinion of the court, wrote: "It is also a most important consideration in the present case, which ought not to be lost sight of, that, supposing these African negroes not to be slaves, but kidnapped and free negroes, the treaty with Spain cannot be obligatory upon them; and the United States are bound to respect their rights as much as those of Spanish subjects. The conflict of rights between the parties under the circumstances, becomes positive and inevitable, and must be decided upon the eternal principles of justice and international law." *The United States v. the Libellants and Claimants of the Schooner Amistad*, 15 Peters 518, 595 (1841).

Justice Story further emphasized the right of these Afrikans to the impartial application of the international law in U.S. courts and to their right to self-determination, as he, in concluding the opinion, noted that the United States no longer insisted upon the Afrikans being delivered to the United States President. He wrote: "[T]here is no ground to assert that the case comes within the purview of the act of 1819, or of any other prohibitory slave trade acts. When Amistad arrived she was in possession of the negroes, asserting their freedom; and in no sense could they possibly intend to import themselves here, as slaves, or for sale as slaves. In this view of the matter, that part of the decree of the District Court is unmaintainable, and must be reversed.

"Upon the whole, our opinion is, that the decree of the Circuit Court, affirming that of the District Court ought to be affirmed, except so far as it directs the negroes to be delivered to the President, to be transported to Africa, in pursuance of the act of the 3rd of March 1819, and, as to this, it ought to be reversed; and that the said negroes be declared to be free, and be dismissed from the custody of the court, and go without day." *Amistad, supra*, 15 Peters, at 596-597.

This development in the law did not, of course, extend the right of self-determination to the two-and-a-half million New Afrikans held as slaves; they were still deemed property.

What it did do was establish the precedent that when kidnapped and enslaved Afrikans are no longer held as slaves, they stand before courts of the U.S. entitled to the free-exercise of choice - self-determined choice - as to their future. It follows that when the Thirteenth Amendment ended slavery - *without* offering U.S. citizenship to the formerly enslaved New Afrikan - the New Afrikan, and all of them, were in the same position as the *Amistad* Afrikans: not slaves "but kidnapped and free" New Afrikans. They were entitled then - and We are entitled now, as heirs to a right never used - to exercise political self-determination.

If it were otherwise - if, in short, the United States could impose U.S. citizenship upon the freed people - then their freedom did not exist. For the touchstone of slavery was that the slavemaster could make the most fundamental decisions, including political ones, *for* the person held as a slave and *without* that person's free and self-determined consent.

It is certain, almost, that the 1883 Supreme Court which proved so hostile to the rights of the freed New Afrikan intended no blanket endorsement of self-determination for New Afrikans. (That court might not have objected to our right to return to Afrika). However, it correctly interpreted the sweep of the Thirteenth Amendment, writing that by *"its own unaided force and effect it abolished slavery, and established universal freedom"* and that the Thirteenth Amendment *"has a reflect character also, establishing and decreeing universal civil and political freedom throughout the United States." The Civil Rights Cases,* 109 U.S. 3, 19 (1883).

I am not aware that the United States Supreme Court or any federal Circuit Court of Appeals has adopted this argument as the law. It is a case for us yet to make. Afrikans, descendants of persons held in the United States as slaves, have no valid U.S. citizenship because few of us have exercised the right to self-determination on the basis of *full* information and without duress of any kind: the free-exercise of self-determination requires that the individual know, first, that he or she possesses the right to self-determination and is entitled to say "no" as well as "yes" to the Fourteenth Amendment's offer of U.S. citizenship. Strategically, this situation offers our people a new vantage point from which to seek and negotiate for whatever are our political (and economic) objectives. This includes our reparation rights.

To sum up, i have argued here that the United States has waged war against us, as individuals and as a nation. (I have deferred the question of whether We are a nation under international law.) My central and underlying point is that our reparations, based upon slavery claims, are best presented in the context of the United States' having denied us the exercise of our right to self-determination.

This is because the most fruitful precedents for our reparations claims are those which have arisen out of the reparations payments and the self-determination arrangements made in settlement of World War I and World War II. It is also because, the fact is, the United States did wage a most heinous war against us.

Permit me to offer this final comment on self-determination and the vitality of the right. A seminar on legal aspects of the struggle against apartheid was held, under the auspices of the United Nations Special Committee Against Apartheid and of the government of Nigeria, from 13 to 16 August 1984, at Lagos. It drew together jurists and social scientists from a number of countries in Afrika, Europe, North America and Asia, representing the principal legal systems of the world. Included was the secretary-general of the International Commission of Jurists. In its concluding, formal Declaration, the Seminar stated:

> The right to self-determination has emerged as part of jus cogens, overriding principles or imperative norms of international law which cannot be set aside by treaty or acquiescence, but only by the formulation of a subsequent norm of the same status to the contrary.

III. NEW AFRIKANS AS A NATION AND THE REPARATIONS PRECEDENTS

It may be possible to devise a strategy designed to win reparations, for slavery-rooted claims, based on damage to the individual, without reference to any group. The Versailles Treaty's assessment of reparations against Germany, at the end of World War I, cites "damage to injured persons and to surviving dependents by personal injury to or death of civilians caused by acts of war" and damages for several other types of injuries to civilians. (Pars. 1-3, 7 & 8 in Annex I, following Article 224 of the Treaty. 2 Bevans 141.) But these damages for reparations were paid to *governments* through the "Reparation Commission" set up by the governments.

The series of World War II treaties and agreements, dealing with reparations, provide for payments "for the rehabilitation and resettlement of non-repatriable victims of German action," but these also flowed through a governmental agency, the Inter-Governmental Committee on Refugees, and by terms of the 14 June 1946 Paris Agreement by the Five Powers "should not be used for the compensation of individual victims but for the rehabilitation and resettlement of persons in eligible classes."

The strongest precedent for individual reparations is the program carried out by the Federal Republic of Germany after World War II. Boris Bittker, in his *The Case for Black Reparations*, *supra*, analyzes the result of the German Reparations laws. Payments did go directly to the individuals (as well as payments made by West Germany to the new state of Israel) for loss of life, impairment of health, deprivation of liberty - including "wearing the Star of David everywhere" - and property and profession. Writing in 1972,

Professor Bittker calculates that "a total of 1,949,470 claims were adjudicated on their merits; 584,703 by German and 1,364,767 by foreign residents." (Presumably most of the foreign residents were Jews who re-settled in Israel.)

Reparations by the United States for the indigenous people here under the Indian Claims Commission Act, Title 25, U.S.C.A., Section 70 et. seq., were not provided to individuals but (Section 70a) to "any Indian tribe, band, or other identifiable group of Indians residing within the territorial limits of the United States or Alaska" for claims in law or equity or sounding in tort, revision of treaties and contracts "on the ground of fraud, duress, unconscionable consideration, mutual or unilateral mistake..." and claims arising from the taking of lands without agreed payment, and for "claims based upon fair and honorable dealings that are not recognized by any existing rule of law or equity."

However, a United States political subdivision, the City of Los Angeles, has paid direct reparations. This was in 1984 to 36 Japanese former city employees who, at the beginning of World War II, had been fired from their jobs and interned, despite being "loyal Americans." The City Council apologized in a resolution and gave each $5,000 as a token reparation. Similarly, the City of San Francisco in January 1983 paid $1,250 per year of internment to former employees of the city who were Japanese.

Finally, Professor Y.N. Kly in his thoughtful book, *International Law and the Black Minority in the U.S.*, suggests that New Afrikans should view self-determination as a last resort and identify ourselves as a "national minority," within the contemplation of the international law, and seek from the United States the "special measures" which the international law requires. Dr. Kly suggests that these "special measures" would make available the circumstances, finances, technology, etc. required to enable the minority to reach equality with the majority, maintain its cultural and ethnic identity, if desired, while sharing a political, economic and social equal-status relationship with the majority." (Page xxiii.) Presumably some of the "finances" of a special measures program could go directly to individuals, although when Dr. Kly chronicles *special measures* programs in a number of states (e.g., the Swedish program for the Lapps), the finances, where this is a part of the program, go to groups. (Pages 23-31.)

Article 27 of the *International Covenant on Civil and Political Rights*, identifies three kinds of "minorities" - ethnic, religious, and linguistic. Dr. Kly believes that since an "ethnic minority" is based not simply on race but on group tradition, or culture, New Afrikans, Puerto Ricans, and Indians could fold themselves within this definition. (Pages xii and 27.)

Whatever the value of this strategy, advocates of achieving reparations as individuals, without reference to group relationship, are apt to find no special encouragement in it.

It is clear, moreover, that the Indian states "in the United States" have been treated (and view themselves) as states and nations, not national minorities. In fact the designation placed upon Indian political units by Justice John Marshall in 1831 - "domestic dependent nations" - remains a part of the law today. Puerto Ricans who have voluntarily come to the United States (it is voluntary only if the effects of colonization are discounted) could be viewed, by those who regard the U.S.'s imposition of citizenship upon the Puerto Ricans as invalid, as a national minority since they are living in another country but have a country of their own. From the standpoint of Puerto Rican nationalists, their country - their state - is *colonized* by the United States, and Puerto Ricans are in a national liberation struggle.

In appraising the situation of New Afrikans in the United States it is important to keep in mind that We have, almost from the beginning, followed simultaneously *three* - not *one* - strategies of struggle. (This is to say that simultaneously *some* of us have followed *each* of the strategies.) Those strategies have been first, to return to Afrika (Paul Cuffee through Garvey to the Hebrew Israelites); second, to change the United States and join it as full citizens (Richard Allen through Frederick Douglass to Martin Luther King), and third, to build an independent state on land claimed in North America by the United States (Gabriel Prosser through Tunis Campbell to Malcolm X and the Provisional Government- RNA). Throughout our three hundred years of struggle on this soil We have, from at least 1660, been evolving into and have become a Black Nation, a New Afrikan nation, even with the simultaneous pursuit of three strategies.

The prolific Floyd J. Miller in his important book, *The Search for A Black Nationality*, found and stated: "A further indication of the depth of this alienation is the fact that at one time or another, almost all black leaders regardless of their reaction to emigration were compelled to acknowledge what both Delaney and Douglass independently announced in the 1850s - that blacks in the United States were a 'nation within a nation.'" [Footnote omitted.]

For clarity on the difference between "nation" and "state" it is perhaps helpful to call on Professor Robin Alison Remington in her discussion of Yugoslavia. She writes: "A country is the piece of real estate occupied by the state. Neither a country nor a state is a 'nation.' Rather, a 'nation' is a group of individuals united by common bonds of historical development, language, religion, and their self-perceived collective identity. *** According to the 1971 census, the Yugoslav population is 20.5 million including five official 'nations' and a variety of nationalities. The nations are the Serbs, 8.4 million; Croats, 4.8 million; Slovenes, 1.7 million; Macedonians, 1.2 million and Montenegrins, 608 thousand."

Elsewhere, i have made a contribution toward (i hope) clarity.

People live in states; The United States is a *state*: all the fifty states make one United States, and in international law the entire United States (with its 50 constituent states) is known as *a* state. A state has people, land and government. The government, acting for the state, protects the people and the land from outside attack by means of diplomacy and its army; government controls conflict among its own people by education and indoctrination and by means of law, courts, and the police. The government, representing the state, has final control over the lives of people. *Only* the state, through its government, can lawfully jail people or kill people - either by executing them or sending people to war.

But people come before states. This is to say that *nations* exist before states. States are created to protect nations. For, a nation is the people and their beliefs and their perspective (their way of looking at themselves and the world) and their way of life - their social structure and their economic structure. These have arisen out of a people's own special history, over time. States can be created suddenly, by declaration, by new constitutions, by military coup and successful revolution and by treaty. But *nations* can only

174

be created by *time: nations are people brought together by common history and common mission and common struggle, cemented by common values and a common way of life, on a given land mass, over time.* Nations must evolve. They come into being by growing over decades.

The United States began as a white nation, a new English nation, which grew up between 1607 and 1776 in a land away from England. In England the people were having a different experience and history than the English in America. In America the Whites, led by the English, fought Indians and Afrikans for that in which they, the Whites, believed: they believed in the superiority of Whites over Indians and Afrikans and the *right* of Whites to take all the land and oppress and exploit Afrikans and Indians.

These *Americans*, the Whites, built a state, a republic, to protect the *American* nation. They did not build this state to protect Indians or Afrikans; in fact, it was built to help Whites better oppress and exploit Indians and Afrikans. It was built to protect the white nation.

Meanwhile, We, the Afrikans, were forming into a new nation also, a new *Afrikan* nation. This happened between 1660, when the English in America decided definitely to hold us in slavery, and 1865, when our work and sacrifice in the Civil War brought an end to slavery. In those two hundred years We who had come from different nations in Afrika, where our states had been weakened or defeated altogether, fused into a new people, a new Afrikan people. Struggle against the oppression of the White nation in North America, the United States, fused us. Over the course of 20 decades.

[DIAGRAM IN ORIGINAL TEXT, NOT REPRODUCED HERE]
STATE STRUCTURE (NEW AFRIKAN NATION; PUERTO RICAN
NATION), SOCIAL STRUCTURE, ECONOMIC STRUCTURE]

THE UNITED STATES, as diagrammed above, typifies the relationship between dominant nation-states and the nations, within, which they dominate. The social structures of the dominated nations remain more or less intact, but these structures are influenced by, and in the final analysis controlled by, the social structure of the dominant nation-state. The dominant nation-state integrates the economy of the dominated nations into its own economic structure. In addition these nations usually are without meaningful state structures and are always completely dominated by the state structure of the dominant nation. (In the United States there are more subordinate nations than the two shown. Principally these are the many Indian nations.)

I have already mentioned some of the state-building efforts undertaken by New Afrikans in North America. What is not commonly acknowledged is that the work of the Richard Allen–Frederick Douglass–Martin King group has also been a form of state-building. For, these men and women were bent on taking the American state-structure, rife with anti-Black laws, and changing it. In other words, they sought to create a state different from that which its White nationalist founders, and the majority of its citizens, really envisioned. With respect to the state structure, it might be added, this strategy has seen some marked success. This success occurred not only because of the work of integrationalists, Martin Luther King and followers, but because of the U.S. government's and white public's reaction to the *independentistas*, Malcolm X, Rap Brown, and their followers, (Yet although discriminatory laws are now gone, since 1968, racism remains in the economic and social structures. Racism also sometimes is operative in the use to which government officials put the state machinery.)

Finally the *Declaration* issued by the international law conference at Lagos in 1984 provided "elements of a definition" of the term "peoples" used in the *Decolonization Declaration, the Declaration of Principles of International Law, and the International Covenants on Human Rights,* in the common phrase, "All peoples have the right of self-determination." According to the 1984 Lagos declaration (Page 6):

    A. The term "people" denotes a social entity possessing a clear identity and its own characteristics;

    B. It implies a relationship with a territory, even if the people in question has been wrongly expelled from it and artificially replaced by another population.

In 1966 the Malcolm X Society, anticipating the founding of a Provisional Government, designated the Five States of Louisiana, Mississippi, Alabama, Georgia, and South Carolina as the national territory of New Afrika, not only because these states were contiguous and fed on the south by the Gulf and on the east by the Atlantic ocean, but especially because these states (plus Virginia) had been the heartland of the territory on which We had developed into a new nation, giving to the land our blood and or sweat, our love and our hopes, during the course of the 200 years between 1660 and 1865, and thereafter.

So the proposition of this paper and the annexed draft reparations legislation is that the United States waged long, cruel, and unjust war against us as a nation, and for that there is responsibility. The World War I and World War II reparations settlements were imposed upon Germany by victorious armies, and Conrad Adenaur, leader of West Germany, engineered the payment of reparations to the Jews as part of the price required of him for loosening the new bonds which bound and humbled the German nation after the war.

Today the New Afrikan nation, still pursuing simultaneously its three strategies of struggle, has no victorious armies to compel compliance, only the international law - and the strength and ingenuity of the uses to which We and or allies may put the politics of the American state. Nevertheless the debt to us and its grounds were clearly presaged by the language and import of the World War I and World War II agreement; only the names need changing:

> -The Allied and Associated Governments affirm and Germany accepts the responsibility of Germany and her allies for causing all the loss and damage to which the allied and Associated Governments and their nationals have been subjected as a consequence of the war imposed upon them by the aggression of Germany and her allies. *Article 231, The Versailles Treaty, 1919.*

> -The Allied and Associated Governments, however, require, and Germany undertakes, that she will make compensation for all damage done to the civilian population of the Allied and Associated Powers and to their property during the period of the belligerency... Article 232, *The Versailles Treaty, 1919.*

-Compensation may be claimed from Germany under Article 232 above in respect of the total damage under the following categories:

(2) Damage caused by Germany or her allies to civilian victims of acts of cruelty, violence, or maltreatment (including injuries to life or health...)

(8) Damage caused to civilians by being forced by Germany or her allies to labour without just remuneration. *Annex 1 to Part VIII, Reparation, in the Versailles Treaty, 1919.*

-Germany must pay in kind for the losses caused by her to the Allied Nations in the course of the war. Reparation is to be received in the first instance by those countries which have borne the main burden of the war ...*Crimea (Yalta) Conference, 1945: German Reparation.*

-In recognition of the fact that large numbers of persons have suffered heavily at the hands of the Nazis and now stand in dire need of aid to promote their rehabilitation ...*Paris Agreement, Reparation From Germany Et Cet., 14 January, 1946, ARTICLE 8.*

-ARTICLE 88. In the portion of Upper Silesia included within the boundaries described below, the inhabitants will be called upon to indicate by a vote whether they wish to be attached to Germany or to Poland.

ANNEX. 2. The plebiscite area shall be immediately placed under the authority of an International Commission ..,

4. The right to vote shall be given to all persons without distinction of sex...The result of the vote will be determined by communes according to the majority of votes in each commune. *Versailles Treaty, 1919.*

In brief, the terms of the attached draft legislation reflect practices which are not unknown to the United States and other states which participated in or observed the arrangements which followed the two world wars. The plan would provide reparations to the state-building Provisional Government but reparations would go, as well, to individuals and to organized, serving, community groups.

IV. Some Policy Considerations

The classic "March on Washington," well-organized and preceded and followed by serious informational and organizational work in the New Afrikan communities across the land can put the issue of *reparations-now* on the general public agenda and create a mass Black bloc in favor of reparations. Further, adroit intervention in the U.S. Presidential and Congressional election processes could yield some members of Congress - perhaps all of Congressman Fauntroy's 120 New Afrikan-dependent Representatives - and a U.S. President generally and provisionally committed to the legislation.

But neither of these necessary achievements is sufficient to win passage of a reparation bill. We need a majority of the 435 members of the U.S. House of Representatives and a majority of the 100 members of the U.S. Senate.

Our problem is the power of lingering racism in the majority of White people in the United States and in their governmental representatives. We should acknowledge that today's America is a different America than 20 years ago: there is considerably less vindictiveness and hostility among young Blacks and Whites, given that Black youth harbor varying degrees of resentment at Whites and their system of preference.

But traditionally there has been a certain meanness in the attitude of most Americans toward us. One wit has opined, "The Americans must really love us, because they've never felt it necessary to say, *"I'm sorry."* Love is not and has not been the issue; justice and payment for stolen labor and the damages of unjust war and cultural assault have been - and are - the issue. It is instructive that when Abraham Lincoln urged by New Afrikan leaders to end slavery at least in Washington, D.C., and the Border States, and motivated by his own complex reasons to do so, including the humanitarian one, moved to end this slavery, he proposed not payment to the Afrikan, for life and labor stolen, but payment to the slaveholders! Payments were made.

To the great credit of the Americans, however, in the blush of the chastening circumstances of a terrible four-year Civil War, the U.S. House of Representatives and the Senate *did* muster a majority in each house and passed a bill, on the Freedman's Bureau, which did provide for us the hallowed *forty acres*. (the houses could not, however, muster the two-thirds majorities in each house needed to override Andrew Johnson's veto, and so the bill did not pass, and We did not get the forty acres.)

Yet despite this and certain other important instances of the triumph of principle, there has also been a consistent counter-trend in the historic relations of White and Black in America, as Derrick Bell has put it in his essay, "The Racial Imperative In American Law," [footnote no. 15]. That trend has been the recurrent sacrifice of justice for New Afrikans to the expedient interests of Whites, even where cost-benefit analysis did not clearly favor those interests. In a related and specific manner, despite the presence of precedents in the Native American and world war reparations settlements, the attitude of the White Community, the Americans, seems to be that freeing us from slavery was enough; *We were lucky to be brought here and lucky to be freed!* These attitudes are obstacles.

I am convinced, however, that collective genius can devise the strategy to win the needed majority In Congress. As a teacher of young people, i am also convinced that part of the strategy must be to alter the textbooks and our conventions in teaching the American experience - and to alter kindred conventions in movies and literature - so that Americans and New Afrikans living now, may come to a deep appreciation of the nature of the war waged against us and Indians in America and of the military occupation We have suffered here, as well as the creative, persistent, courageous and often brilliant struggle Indians and New Afrikans have waged in response.

In the end, history makes clear that to win reparations We must be prepared to take this righteous struggle into the streets. We must be prepared to stop all the machinery of America. If need be, until the just debt of reparations is paid.

FREE THE LAND!

A Proposed Act Submitted To Some Members of Congress
In September and October 1987

Submitted by:
Dr. Imari Abubakari Obadele
President, Republic of New Afrika
Assistant Professor, The College of Wooster

Attorney Chokwe Lumumba, Chairperson
The New Afrikan People's Organization

AN ACT TO STIMULATE ECONOMIC GROWTH IN THE UNITED STATES AND COMPENSATE, IN PART, FOR THE GRIEVOUS WRONGS OF SLAVERY AND THE UNJUST ENRICHMENT WHICH ACCRUED TO THE UNITED STATES THEREFROM

Preamble

WHEREAS the Congress of the United States has never accorded ultimate political justice to New Afrikans in this country - New Afrikans being all the descendants of Afrikans held as slaves in this country - by authorizing a plebiscite and a process of registration whereby collectively and individually New Afrikans could exercise their right to self-determination by freely and with full information voting collectively on their future, and registering individual political options, and

WHEREAS the Congress of the United States recognizes the Thirteenth Amendment as protecting this right of New Afrikan people to self-determination, and

WHEREAS the illegal transportation to, and the enslavement of Afrikan people in the United States was carried out under authority of the U.S. Constitution for seventy-seven years, and for a total of 200 years under the antecedent authority of the Articles of Confederation, and the Colonial law, and

WHEREAS the authority in the United States Constitution for enslavement of the New Afrikan people was contained in clause three, Section Two of the Fourth Article, commonly known as the fugitive slave provision, which placed the full force of the United States military, executives, and courts against even the most inoffensive person held as a slave who quietly slipped away to freedom, and against the entire New Afrikan people, and

WHEREAS the United States further dehumanized the New Afrikan by holding her/him to have the status of three-fifths of a white person in clause three, Section Two of Article One of the U.S. Constitution, and

WHEREAS that most heinous war against Afrika, commonly known as the slave trade, was authorized for United States principals for 20 years more after the ratification of the United States' Constitution by clause one in Section Nine of the First Article of the United States Constitution, and

WHEREAS principles of international law and a reconciliation of the peoples require that the United States attempt a good faith, if partial, reparation for the unjust war waged against the New Afrikan people for 200 years, and for cultural destruction, and for labor stolen, and

WHEREAS the concept of reparations is recognized in United States law, and the United States has sponsored and paid reparations for other victims, and

WHEREAS the Congress finds that New Afrikan people, descendants of persons kidnapped from Afrika and held here against their will currently residing in the United States, are entitled to exercise collective and individual rights to self-determination, and

WHEREAS the Congress is aware that the options regarding political future which are open to the New Afrikans include (a) return to Afrika, (b) departure for some country other than one in Afrika, (c) acceptance of U.S. citizenship, and (d) creation of an independent New Afrikan state in North America, and

WHEREAS the Congress finds that various international covenants and resolutions affirming that all peoples have the right to self-determination apply to Afrikan people born in North America, and

WHEREAS the Congress recognizes that the necessary foundation for effectuating the results of an act of self-determination by the New Afrikan people is the means and resources to achieve those results, and

WHEREAS the authority for providing such means and resources lies in Section Two of the Thirteenth Amendment, and

WHEREAS this legislation affects only those parties under domestic United States jurisdiction and is not to be construed as discharging the obligation owed to Afrikan people by other countries and governments,

THEREFORE the following provisions are enacted into law under the authority of the Thirteenth Amendment to the United States Constitution.

Title I. Reparations

1. The United States accepts the obligation of the United States to pay reparations to the descendants of Afrikans held as slaves in the United States and undertakes to make such payment to the New Afrikan nation as political unit, to compensate in part for the destruction and/or damage to Afrikan political units in Afrika and for the abortion and the destruction of New Afrikan political units in the United States during the era of slavery, and payments to New Afrikan organizations to compensate in part for the deliberate subversion of the New Afrikan social structure, and the obligation to pay directly to each New Afrikan, descendant of Afrikans held as slaves in the United States and born on or before the date of ratification of this Act and still living on the date of each appropriation, the total sum of _____ dollars.

2. Congress is authorized to appropriate and pay annually sums of money and credit to discharge this obligation over a period of years, not less than three-billion dollars annually.

    a. One-third of the annual sums shall go directly to each individual, except that the sum due a person not yet 17 years of age who is not the head of an independent household shall be paid to the head-of-household who stands as such person's parent or guardian or jointly to such persons in the case of husband and wife. Social Security records, Internal Revenue Service records, and Aid to Dependent-Children records, or records of successor agencies, shall be available to facilitate determination of heads-of-household, as consistently as possible with the provisions of the Privacy Act, its conflicting provisions hereby being waived. This program shall be administered by the Internal Revenue Service.

One-third of the annual sum shall go directly to the duly elected government of the Republic of New Afrika, and to any other state-building entity of New Afrikan people, provided that elections for the RNA Provisional Government or for the officers of such other New Afrikan state-holding entity are observed by the United Nations or other distinguished international body and deemed by said international body to be open, honest, and democratic, for purposes of the economic, social, cultural, and educational development of the New Afrikan nation-state or states. This payment shall be made by the United States Treasury.

c. One-third of the annual sum shall be paid directly to a National Congress of Organizations, consisting of all the New Afrikan churches and other New Afrikan organizations which for a period of two years prior to the enactment of this legislation have engaged in community programs designed to end the scourge of drugs and crime in New Afrikan communities and advance the social, economic, educational, or cultural progress and enrichment of New Afrikan people. Programs serving New Afrikan communities shall be eligible to participate in local conventions of the National Congress of Organizations, provided that these programs are led by New Afrikans and have been so led for at least three years prior to enactment of this legislation. The United States Treasury shall administer this payment.

Title II - Plebiscites & Self-Determination

Pursuant to the Thirteenth Amendment, the United States President is authorized and directed to arrange with the President or appropriate body of the Provisional Government of the Republic of New Afrika and/or other state-building entity the holding, within five years after the enactment of this legislation, of independence plebiscites in all such counties or major portions of such counties in the streets of South Carolina, Georgia, Florida, Alabama, Mississippi, Louisiana, Arkansas, and Tennessee, where ten percent of Afrikans, aged 16 or over, within such counties or major portions thereof signify their desire for the holding of such plebiscites.

1. Such ten-percent petitions may be certified by special Status Courts, hereby created in the same districts as the now-established districts for United States courts, within the states enumerated in Paragraph One of this Title, and Regional Status

Courts are hereby created in New York, Chicago, Atlanta, and Los Angeles. The judges of these Article One–Thirteenth *Amendment Status Courts* shall be three in number: one appointed by the President of the United States, one appointed by the Republic of New Afrika, and one which the General Assembly of the United Nations shall be invited to appoint.

2. The jurisdiction of said Status Courts shall be limited to (1) determination of the validity of petitions for plebiscites and their certification, (2) the certification of Election results, and (3) such other matters as are set out in this Act. Such Status Courts, established under Article One and the Thirteenth and Fourteenth Amendments of the United States Constitution, and the agreement of the Provisional Government of the Republic of New Afrika insofar as the authority of the United States is concerned, shall have power to compel the appearance and testimony of witnesses, issue process for production of evidence, make findings of fact and conclusions of law, conduct trials, and issue judgments.

3. Such Status Courts shall have power through a conference, presided over by a Chief Judge elected by the Conference of all Status Court judges, to issue rules, consistent with the rules of the federal courts of the United States, the Judicial Statute of the Republic of New Afrika, and the Statute of the International Court of Justice. Such rule shall become effective if not returned for further consideration by the United States or the Republic of New Afrika sixty days after the date

of promulgation by the Chief Judge of the Status Courts. In the event of such return, the Chief Judge may amend the Rules and promulgate them de novo, under the same conditions of veto. Judges of the Status Courts shall have power to conduct contempt proceedings and assess penalties upon findings of contempt, which penalties should not exceed five years in prison and a $10,000 fine.

4. Compensation for Status Court judges shall be the same as that of District Judges of the United States. The United States shall promptly and regularly pay these salaries and provide for adequate staffing and support services for the Status Courts. Such compensation and expenses shall be included in the regular budgeting and appropriations for the U.S. Courts and shall not be treated as a charge against the appropriation for reparations.

5. Change of Sovereignty. Whenever a simple majority of voters in a county or a portion of a county pre-designated for plebiscite, shall during a plebiscite on status vote in favor of a majority of Republic of New Afrikan candidates for the legislature or governing body of such county, or a portion thereof, that area shall be deemed to be under the sovereignty of the Republic of New Afrika. The provisions of this Section, paragraphs 6,7 and 8 apply not only to the RNA Provisional Government but to any New Afrikan state-building entity filing ten-percent petitions in accordance with paragraphs 1 through 5 of Title II of this act.

6. The United States shall undertake to secure agreement from the Republic of New Afrika that all

persons residing in an area where the Republic of New Afrika wins sovereignty shall be guaranteed all the rights set forth in the United Nations Covenant on Civil and Political Rights, to the same extent that the United States guarantees these rights to all persons residing in the United States.

7. Immediately after the first plebiscite which results in a confirmation of Republic of New Afrika sovereignty, the President of the United States shall invite the President of the Republic of New Afrika and the Secretary General of the United Nations to join in a request to the Status Court that they open official *Status Registers*. These *Registers* shall permit individual New Afrikans who, living in the United states, do not wish to accept United States citizenship, and New Afrikans who, living in New Afrika, do not wish to retain New Afrikan citizenship, to register these personal options. A New Afrikan who does not register a personal option shall be deemed to have the citizenship of the sovereignty - New Afrikan or United States - under which he or she lives, but this fact for New Afrikans who remain in the United States does not obliterate New Afrikan citizenship in the context of dual citizenship. Such registration of personal choice must take place within three years of a status plebiscite in the area in which a person resides, where a change of sovereignty occurs. In all cases New Afrikans wishing to exercise a personal option for citizenship in the Republic of New Afrika but living in an area where no plebiscite has been held or where no status court is established, must do so within ten years after the date of the enactment

of this legislation. For this purpose the United States Postal Service shall provide secure *Status Letters* which, after execution, shall be delivered to the appropriate Regional Status Courts in New York, Chicago, Atlanta, or Los Angeles. Persons may file personally at these Regional Status courts. The citizenship of a child, 15-years-old or younger, shall be the same as that of his or her parents, parent, or guardian who stands as head-of-household, unless such person maintains an independent household.

Title III - Freedom for Black Liberation Army Soldiers

1. The Congress of the United States finds that the continued imprisonment of the following Black Liberation Army soldiers and certain other persons is contrary to the national interests of the United States and a substantial impediment to the successful fulfillment of the intent of this legislation under the Thirteenth Amendment, that intent being to stimulate economic growth in the United States, compensate in part victims and heirs for past wrongs, facilitate racial healing and reconciliation in the United States, and provide for the long-delayed exercise of the right to self-determination by the New Afrikan people. The Congress finds that the Continued imprisonment of these persons is contrary to fulfillment of United States obligations under the Thirteenth Amendment. The Congress therefore directs the immediate release of these persons from prison without condition:

Sundiata Acoli
Assata Shakur
Herman Bell
Albert Nuh Washington
Jalil Muntaqim
Geronimo JiJaga (Pratt)
Mutulu Shakur
Dhoruba Bin Wahad
Kubwa Obadele
Kwablah Mthawabu
Sekou Odinga
Veronza Bowers
Atiba Shanna
Bashir Hameed
Abdul Majid
Haroun Abdul Rauf

2. The United States Congress, for its part, further provides to the Status Courts, hereinabove established, jurisdiction to accept applications from persons similarly situated and the power to make prompt and just decisions on their application for release.

Title IV - Administrative Funds

Funds for the administration of the provisions of the Act shall be appropriated from the general treasury of the United States and included in the budgets of the Status Courts and the executive agencies responsible for carrying out the provisions of this legislation, without any charges against the sums appropriated for the payment of reparations under Title I of this Act.

NOTES:

Text of The Civil Liberties Act of 1988 which granted reparations to Japanese Americans, passed by the U.S. Congress 10 August 1988, Public Law 100-383, 100th Congress
Reprinted in original Reparations Yes text, but not included herein

Text of H.R. 40
103rd Congress, 1st Session
January 1993
Reprinted in original Reparations Yes text, but not included herein

Queen Mother Audley Moore

Chokwe Lumumba with Taifa, 1994

Imari Obadele with Taifa,
ca.1976

Imari Obadele with Taifa,
ca. 1980

Taifa with Chokwe Lumumba,
ca. 2010

Queen Mother Moore with Taifa, 1994

Queen Mother Moore with Taifa, ca. 1989

Congressman John Conyers with Taifa, 2015

Taifa with Congresswoman Sheila Jackson Lee, 2022

INDEX

A

Abott, Diane – 98

Abubakari, Dara – 49

Accra, Ghana Reparations and Racial Healing Summit – 98

Achiume, Tendayi – 19

ACLU – 11

Adebayo, Dr. Marsha Coleman – 84

Aetna – 75

Afoh, Kwame – 49

African American Redress Network – 11, 65-66, 84

African National Reparations Organization – 34,36

African People's Socialist Party – 34,37

Afrik, Hannibal – 49

AIG – 75

Aiwuyor, Jessica Ann Mitchell – 54, 105

Aiyetoro, Attorney Adjoa – 34, 37, 41, 43, 55

Akufo-Addo, Nana – 98

Alexander, Rev. Aundreia – 81

Alexander, Erika – 10, 64, 116

Alghanee, Njeri – 49

Ali, Hodari – 49

Alston, Christopher – 49

Amalgamated Bank – 18, 44, 76

America, Dr. Richard – 34

American Constitution Society for Law and Policy – 89

American Descendants of Slavery – 62

Anti-Depression Program – 26, 33

Arbery, Ahmaud – 28

Arikpo, Earline – 49

Asheville, North Carolina – 45, 66, 72

Association of Black Psychologists – 58

Austin-Hillery, Nicole – 24

B

Bachelet, Michelle – 95-96

Bahamas – 98

Baltimore Sun – 79

Bank of America – 75-76

Baptiste, Judge Lionel Jean – 63

Barbados – 45,96

Barron, Assemblyman Charles – 40,51

Batrice, Raina – 44

Beckles, Vice Chancellor Sir Hilary – 97, 100

Ben & Jerry's Ice Cream – 18, 44, 75-76

Berry, Dr. Mary Frances – 40

Bethel AME Church – 84
Bethesda Moses African
    Cemetery - 67
Bethune, Mary McLeod – 88
Biden, President Joe – 5, 24, 61
Big Payback, The – 10, 64, 116
Bill of Rights for the
    Disadvantaged – 32
Bishop, Maurice – 96
Black Belt Justice Center – 85
Black Codes – 6, 31
Black Farmers – 85
Black Liberation Movement –
    13
Black Lives Matter – 25
Black Manifesto – 26, 33
Black Nationalist – 9, 30, 32,
    34, 38, 79
Black Panther Party – 15, 26,
    33,37, 63
Black Reparations Commission
    – 36-37
Black/white wealth gap – 6, 36,
    110, 117
Booker, Senator Cory – 23, 26,
    44
Boston Globe – 79
Bowles, Will – 67
Bowman, Representative Jamal
    – 19
Braithwaite, Alderman Peter –
    63
Brath, Elombe – 37
Braxton, Rev. Dr. JoAnne – 84

Britain's Black Debt:
    Reparations for
    Caribbean Slavery
    and Native Genocide
    - 97
Bruce's Beach – 82, 84, 106
Bruce, Willa and Charles – 82
Burge, John – 93
Burnham, Judge Margaret – 84
Burns, Attorney Haywood – 37

C

Cabral, Amilcar – 109
California – 13, 17, 30, 37, 40,
    45, 50, 61, 68-69, 82
California Interim Report –
    59, 60-61, 69
California Reparations Task
    Force – 30, 52, 54-55,
    57-58, 61, 69
Canadian National – 75
Cannabis Industry – 45, 63-64
CARICOM Reparations
    Commission (CRC)
    – 63-64, 87, 97,
    100-104
Castile, Philando – 95
Central York (Pennsylvania)
    School District – 24
Chappelle, Dave – 10
Chattahoochee Brick
    Company – 67, 83

Chicago City Council
    Reparations
    Ordinance – 45, 70,
    94
Chicago Police Torture – 45,
70, 93-94
Chinweizu, Professor – 100,
    110
Civil Rights Congress – 87
Clotilda – 83
Clubhouse – 58
Coates, Ta-Nehisi – 8-9, 11,
    22, 25, 31
Cohen, Chairman Steve –
    19-22
COINTELPRO – 37, 44, 112
Color of Change – 19, 21, 78
Columbia Law School – 30,
    57, 84
Commission to Quantify the Debt
    Owed to African
    Americans – 40
Commission to Study and
    Develop Reparations
    Proposals for African
    Americans Act – 23
Commission to Study
    Reparations Proposals for
    African Americans Act –
    39
Comprehensive Reparations
    – 105-106
Convict Leasing – 6, 31, 67,
    83

Conyers, Representative
    John - 9, 19, 27-28,
    38-39, 43, 49, 52
COVID-19 –25, 53-54, 64,
    75, 81
Crimes Against Humanity –
    88, 97, 101
Criminal Punishment
    System – 29, 92, 111
Crockett, Judge George – 88
CSX – 75

D

Daniels, Dr. Ron – 19-20, 43,
    63
DC Compensated
    Emancipation Act – 17
December 12th Movement –
    34
Deen, Mickey – 67
Delta Sigma Theta – 40
Dickerson, Rev. Isaiah – 32, 49
Du Bois, W.E.B. – 88

E

Elaine, Arkansas – 16, 83
Elorza, Rhode Island Mayor
    Jorge O. – 73
Emotional Emancipation
    Circles – 58
England's Royal Family – 98
Episcopal Church – 44

Episcopal Diocese of Maryland
  – 44, 81
Ethiopian Women's
  Organization – 87
Evanston, Illinois – 13, 17,
  40, 45, 51, 62-66, 68,
  70, 116
E.W. Scripps – 75, 77
Executive Order – 5, 7, 24,
  52, 60, 73

F

Farmer, Professor Ashley – 88
Farmer-Paellmann, Deadria –
  41, 76
Federal Bureau of
  Investigation - 112
Ferguson, Herman – 49
First Repair – 62-63, 65
Fischer, Mayor Greg –71
Fleet Boston Financial Group
  – 75
Floyd, George – 9-10, 23, 25,
  28, 44, 61, 77, 95, 99
Forman, James – 26, 33, 81
Forty (40) acres and a mule –
  21-22, 27, 31, 33, 39
Foundational Black
  Americans – 62
Fourteenth (14th)
  Amendment– 35

Franklin, V.P. – 67
Freedmen –59, 62
Freeman, Bridget –100
Free Press – 77
Fugitive Slave Act – 7, 62

G

Gannett – 75, 77
Garcetti, Mayor Eric – 69
Garvey, Marcus – 32, 49, 96,
  112
Geneva, Switzerland – 90-91,
  93-95
Genocide – 32, 87-90, 92,
  94,96-97, 99-102, 104,
  113
Genocide Convention – 87-90
Georgetown University –
  30, 79, 109
Germany – 98
Gerrymandering – 31
Gill, Arley – 97
G.I. Bill – 31, 51
Glover, Danny – 22, 62-64
Glover, Donald – 116
Great Britain – 99
Greenwood Foundation – 85
Grenada –97-98
Grills, Dr. Cheryl – 58
GU-272 – 79, 106

H

Haight, Judge Charles – 90
Haiti – 17, 35, 45, 99
Hannah-Jones, Nikole
        – 8-9, 11, 25, 31
Hansford, Professor
        Justin – 93
Harper, Councilwoman
        Vanessa Hall – 63
Hartford Courant – 79
Harvard Law School – 30, 34
Harvard Medical School
        Lancet Commission
        on Reparations
        and Redistributive
        Justice – 76
Haygood, Ryan – 50
Heath, Dreisen – 19-20, 44
Henry, Kennis – 44
Hill, Sylvia – 37
Hinds, Attorney Lennox –
        90-91
Hollywood – 10, 116
Homestead Act – 31
House, Callie – 21, 32, 49,
        112
House of Representatives
        – 5, 20, 22, 46
Howard, Kamm – 19, 21-22,
        24, 43, 63
Howard University – 8, 15,
        30, 65, 84, 94, 103
Howlett Family – 80
H.R. 40 – 7, 9-10, 19-23, 27,
        39-40, 43, 45, 50, 52,
        60-61, 63-64, 76, 80,
        116
H. Res. 194 – 22
Human Rights Watch – 11,
        19-20, 24, 44

I

Inter-American Commission
        on Human Rights –
        30, 92, 94

J

Jamaica – 32, 45, 98-99
James, C.L.R. – 96
January 6 Capitol
        Insurrection
        – 25, 81
Japanese American Civil
        Liberties Act – 38
Japanese Americans – 27, 38,
        112
Jesuits – 44, 79, 109

K

Kefing, Omowale – 49
Killingham, Marilyn – 49
King, Regina – 116
Kirksey, MS State Senator
        Henry – 37
Knight Ridder – 75
Kuumba, Nia – 49

L

Lakeland Community
Heritage
Project – 84
Lammy, David – 98

Lee, Congresswoman Sheila
    Jackson – 10, 18-20,
    22-23, 43, 62-64, 67,
    75, 116
Legacy Coalition – 84
Lewis, Dorothy Benton – 12,
    36-37, 40, 43, 49
Lineage-based Standard –
    53-54, 106
Litigation Strategies Committee
    – 41
Lumumba, Chokwe – 12, 26
    34, 37, 49, 87, 90, 109

M

McConnell, Senator Mitch – 20
McCurty, Tracy – 85
McDougall, Attorney Gay –
    37, 92
McGriff, Milton – 49
McIntyre, Charshee – 49
McKay, Claude – 96
McSpadden, Leslie – 93
MAAFA – 75, 103, 105
Malcolm X – 32, 34, 82, 107
Malveaux, Dr. Julianne – 23,
    63
Manhattan Bank – 75
Marley, Bob – 96
Martin, Trayvon – 77
Masaoka, Kathy – 19
Marable, Dr. Manning – 37
Mason, Dame Sandra – 96
Media 2070 – 77-79
Moore, Kamilah – 57-58

Moore, Queen Mother
    Audley 12, 26, 32, 49,
    87-88,
Movement 4 Black Lives – 11,
    44
Muhammad, Aisha – 37
Muhammad, Askia – 37
Muhammad, Elijah –49

N

NAACP – 40, 50, 63
Nabors, Rev. Dr. Michael – 63
Namibia – 98
Nanny, Queen – 96
National African American
    Reparations Commission
    (NAARC) – 11, 19, 43,
    53, 62-65, 67 81, 102-103,
    105, 111-112
National Alliance Against
    Racist and Political
    Repression – 92
National Assembly of American
    Slavery Descendants
    (NAASD) – 57
National Association of Black
    Political Scientists – 40
National Association of Black
    Social Workers – 40
National Bar Association – 40
National Black Cultural
    Information Trust
    (NBCIT) – 105
National Black Economic
Development Conference – 33

National Black Political Convention (Gary, IN) – 33

National Black United Front – 34, 87, 92

National Coalition of Blacks for Reparations in America (N'COBRA) – 11, 19, 24, 26-27, 34, 38-41, 43-44, 53, 63, 65, 87, 103, 111, 115

N'COBRA Legislative Commission – 39, 44

National Conference of Black Lawyers (NCBL) – 34, 37, 40

National Council of Churches – 44, 80-81

National Ex-Slave Mutual Relief Bounty and Pension Association – 32

Nation of Islam – 33, 37

Network Lobby for Catholic Social Justice – 41, 81

New Afrikan Independence Movement – 13, 34, 36, 82

New Afrikan Political Science – 35

New Afrikans – 35, 37

New Jersey Institute for Social Justice – 50

New Jersey State Reparations Bill – 51, 72

Newsom, Governor Gavin – 52, 58, 69

New York Life – 75

New York State Community Commission on Reparations – 51

Nigeria – 100, 110

Norfolk Southern – 75

Northeastern University Civil Rights and Restorative Justice Project – 84

Novak, Mary J. – 81

O

Obadele, Imari Abubakari I – 12-13, 26, 28, 34, 36-38, 43, 49, 87, 91, 110, 112

Obadele, Johnita – 43

Obafemi, Ahmed – 37, 49

Ocoee, Florida – 83

Ogletree, Professor Charles – 22, 92

Old Executive Office Building – 80

Olusegun, Kalonji (Vince Godwin) – 37, 43, 49

Olusegun, Kupenda – 43

Oprah – 114

Owens, MA State Senator Bill 39, 49

P

Parks, Rosa – 87
Patterson, William – 87-88
Phillips, Eric – 63
Players Coalition – 17, 44
Political Prisoners – 36,
    90-92, 96, 111-112
Prisoners of War – 36, 90-92,
    111-113
Providence Bank of Rhode
    Island – 76

R

Rabb, PA State
    Representative
    Chris – 73
Race and the Constitution
    Forum – 34
Reagan, President Ronald –
    8, 89
Redlining – 6, 31, 70
Religious Action Center of
    Reform Judaism – 44
Reparations Finance Lab – 67
"Reparations Ray" Jenkins –
    38, 49
Reparations Yes! – 9, 25-26,
    35-36
Reparatory Justice – 7, 11, 26,
    35, 48-49, 57, 66, 70,
    97, 101, 103, 105,
    110-111, 113-115, 117
Repatriation – 11, 102-103,
    111, 115
Republic of New Afrika (RNA)
    26, 33, 36, 49, 91

Restitution – 15, 21, 47, 60, 76,
    94, 104-105, 115
Robeson, Paul – 88
Robinson, Dino – 65
Robinson, Randall – 31, 40
Robinson, Rashad – 19, 21
Rodney, Walter – 96
Rosewood, Florida – 16, 41, 70
Royall, Belinda Sutton – 31, 49
Ryan, April –21-22

S

S. 40 – 23, 44, 52
Saint Lucia – 98
Saint Vincent and the
    Grenadines – 98
Salim, Salim Ahmed – 91
Sanchez, Sonia – 37
Satterwhite, Omowale – 37
Scott, Dred – 113-114
Scott, MacKenzie – 100
Seale, Bobby – 37
Self-determination –6, 32,
    35-36, 51, 57, 79, 87, 91
Seneca Village – 84
Shakur, Mutulu – 90
Sharecropping System – 6, 31,
    51
Shelton, Hilary –19
Sherman, General – 21-22, 28
Shorefront Legacy Center – 65
Sigma Gamma Ro – 40
Simmons, Alderman Robin
    Rue – 10, 62-65, 118

Simmons, Damario Solomon
— 85
Slavery Disclosure
Ordinances – 45
Smith, Kemba – 92
Snyder, Rev. Dale – 84
Spain – 99
Special Field Order #15 – 31
Spirit of Mandela
International
Tribunal – 95-96
Sutton, Bishop Eugene – 81

T

Taylor, Breonna – 10, 25, 28,
77, 96, 99
TEDx Talk – 18
Terrell, Mary Church – 88
Thirteenth (13th)
Amendment – 34,
47, 113
Thurgood Marshall Civil
Rights Center – 65,
84, 94
Till, Emmett – 83
Till-Mobley, Mamie – 83, 93
TransAtlantic Slave Trade –
71, 75, 81, 99
Tribune – 75, 77
Trump, Donald – 10, 44

Tulsa, Oklahoma – 10, 16, 63,
66, 73, 85
Tulsa Race Massacre – 10, 73,
85, 106

U

Underwood, William – 27
Union Pacific – 75
Union for Reform Judaism – 44
United Church of Christ –
44, 80, 92
United Kingdom – 80, 97-98
United Nations (UN) – 87, 91
UN Committee Against Torture
– 93-94
UN Convention Against Torture
– 93
UN General Assembly – 47, 60,
88, 91, 104
UN High Commissioner for
Human Rights – 95
UN Human Rights Commission
– 92
UN Human Rights Council
–95
United States Constitution – 7,
24, 34, 113
Universal Negro
Improvement
Association – 32

Universities Studying
  Slavery - 79
University of Virginia – 74,
  80
University of the West
  Indies –97, 100
U.S. Conference of Mayors
  –17, 44
U.S. Human Rights
  Network –95
U.S. Senate – 23-24, 44-46,
  89
Urgent Debate on Racism
  and Police
  Brutality – 95

V

Vesey, Denmark – 6
Virginia Episcopal Diocese
  - 44

W

Wald, Judge Patricia – 92
Walters, Dr. Ron – 37, 49
Warfield-Coppock, Nzinga – 37
Watchmen - 10, 116
Weber, Shirley – 19, 52
We Charge Genocide Historic
  Petition – 87, 89, 94
West and the Rest of Us, The –
  100, 110
Where Is My Land? – 83
Why We Can't Wait Coalition - 5
Wilkins, Henry – 63
Williams, Dr. K. Karen – 67
Williams, Enith Martin – 67
Willow Oaks Country Club – 80
Wilmington, North Carolina – 16,
  41, 70, 78, 83
Winbush, Professor Raymond – 40
Winkler, Jim – 81

OTHER BOOKS BY NKECHI

Taifa describes her best-seller memoir
***Black Power, Black Lawyer: My
Audacious Quest for Justice*** as
"part memoir, part textbook, part study
guide, and part expose! It teaches,
preaches, rhapsodizes, and tantalizes,
stitching suspense, calamity, humor
and wit into a tapestry of history,
politics, law, culture and romance.

A master storyteller, Taifa is the author of three classics
for children: ***Shining Legacy, The Adventures of Kojo
and Ama***, and ***Three Tales of Wisdom***

Scan codes to see all books by Nkechi on AALBC & AMAZON

DYNAMO EVENT SPEAKER!

Let Nkechi Taifa help empower your institution, company or membership as your next Convention or Commencement Speaker, Keynote Address, University or College Lecture, or MC!

Taifa's motivational speaking is captivating. Her customized, innovative and interactive presentations are accentuated by her high energy and creative style.

Scan the Qr Code to learn more about Nkechi's speaking events.

"As the granddaughter of a lynching victim, I was truly blown away by your speech on reparations, and quite frankly have NEVER heard a more compelling explanation and historical presentation! I believe it is a message everyone should and must hear!"
**CRYSTAL CHARLEY-SIBLEY, NAACP
NJ STATE CONFERENCE CONVENTION CHAIR**

"Taifa is blessed with the rare ability to connect with leaders and constituencies from a broad range of circles, from community-based, grassroots organizations, to the halls of Congress to the White House in pursuit of a righteous cause."
**RON DANIELS, CONVENER,
NATIONAL AFRICAN AMERICAN
REPARATIONS COMMISSION**

Nkechi Taifa is a civil and human rights attorney, scholar-activist, and author. She is president of The Taifa Group LLC, founder and director of the Reparation Education Project Inc., and serves as Senior Fellow for the Center of Justice at Columbia University and as a 2023 Harvard Kennedy School scholar. A visionary thought leader and nationally recognized expert and commentator on race and justice issues, Nkechi is convener emeritus of the Justice Roundtable, and has served as an appointed Commissioner and Chair of the D.C. Commission on Human Rights.

Over the course of her career, she has worked for the Open Society Foundations, Howard University School of Law, the American Civil Liberties Union, Women's Legal Defense Fund, National Prison Project, as an attorney in private practice, and a first-grade teacher. Taifa is an inaugural Commissioner on the National African American Reparations Commission, and a founder of the National Coalition of Blacks for Reparations in America. She has testified on the issue of reparations before the United States Congress, the Inter-American Commission on Human Rights, the U.S Helsinki Commission, the California Reparations Task Force, the DC City Council, and the Maryland Legislature. A native Washingtonian, Nkechi is the author of the best-selling memoir, *Black Power, Black Lawyer: My Audacious Quest for Justice*, as well as several books for children. www.NkechiTaifa.org.

Made in the USA
Middletown, DE
06 November 2023

42028049R00125